Return to Manitou

RETURN TO MANITOU

Nancy J. Bailey

Return to Manitou

All Rights Reserved. Copyright © 2009 Nancy J. Bailey

Second Edition

No part of this book may be reproduced or transmitted in any form or by any means, graphic, electronic, or mechanical, including photocopying, recording, taping, or by any information storage or retrieval system, without the permission in writing from the publisher.

Published by Nancy J. Bailey

ISBN: 1449914004

Printed in the United States of America

Cover Photo of Kerry Airatude at Clifford's Bay

© 2004 Frank Aben

Illustrations © 2004 Nancy J. Bailey

Other Books by Nancy J. Bailey

Clifford of Drummond Island

Holding the Ladder

My Best Cat

The Horses Who Inspired Me

For Kimmy

Preface

Fisher was a small animal, but a great hunter. One day the cold became too much, so he told his friends, Otter, Lynx and Wolverine, "We will go where the Earth is closest to Skyland. The Skyland is always warm, and we will bring some of the warmth down to Earth."

They traveled far up in the mountains, closer and closer to Skyland. When they were close, Fisher said, "We must jump up and break through to the land above the sky."

Otter jumped, bumped his head on the sky, and fell back down the mountain.

Lynx jumped, bumped his head and became unconscious.

Wolverine jumped, bumped his head and kept jumping over and over until the sky cracked a little, then finally it broke open.

Fisher jumped through after him and found the place to be absolutely beautiful and warm. Birds flew through the crack in the sky to the world down below. The warmth began to flow to the Earth and melt the snow.

The Sky-People saw the warmth escaping and called out, "Thieves!"

Wolverine ran back to the crack in the sky, but Fisher was making the crack bigger. Arrows were flying through the air. Fisher was killed.

The Great Spirit, Gitchee Manitou, took pity on Fisher, healing him and placing him in the sky forever, where he became the Big Dipper.

Each Autumn, as Fisher falls toward the Earth, the Sky-People try to patch the crack and Winter arrives. Then in the Spring, Fisher climbs to the sky and reopens the crack -- and Summer again warms the Earth.

~ Native American Legend

Acknowledgements

To Scorch, who makes sure I am never alone.

To Walli Bellairs, who has provided me with a stunning example of true reliability, not to mention generosity. Thank you so much – you are one in a million.

Thank you Amanda for encouraging me to, "Stick with it!"

With special gratitude to my "horse whisperer", Jacki Rodosalewicz.

To my beautiful cousin Mary Jo, who exemplifies everything I am trying to say with this story.

To my longtime friend Rita Heydon, who has thrown me a lifeline more than once.

Thanks Ted for your faith in me.

Thank you Sandy Crechiolo for your help with Zach, and for all your support.

To Gina and Logan Hyatt who are always there for me.

To veterinarians Doreen Cawley, Cheryl Smith, and Anne Hale – where would we be without you?

To Nicole; thank you for your gift of friendship. You are a "rare find!"

To my friend Steve Stanchfield who has taught me, without criticism, that I can be more and expect more.

Thank you Ellen, for your loyalty and generosity.

Thanks Bill and Chris for your love and support.

Janice, thank you for the prayers.

With gratitude to Melissa Muldoon for your ready laugh and steadfast optimism.

Thank you Susan Sanchez for the gift of Aldie.

Frank Aben, thanks for sharing your time and talent to help make this beautiful book cover.

To my greatest supporters of the Clifford book: The Michigan Justin Morgan Horse Association and the citizens of Drummond Island.

To Mom and Dad for their pride and support of the whole Clifford endeavor.

To Clifford, Trudy and Cajun, big hugs and kisses.

And special thanks to my heavenly Father, who always provides a way.

Chapter One

"The perception of beauty is a moral test."
~ Henry David Thoreau

I had never liked my nose. I thought it was too wide and the nostrils too large. It was bulbous and out of proportion with my face. If I'd had huge lips like Julia Roberts or eyes like Goldie Hawn, then maybe the nose would have been okay, because other features would have balanced it all out. But I didn't have movie star features. The nose was just too big.

I didn't spend a lot of time thinking about it. I spent many hours in the woods, especially in the summer, and when I was in the woods my appearance didn't matter at all. I had taken to hitching my mare to a cart and driving her along the back roads at a blistering pace, yelling and laughing as we flew over bumps and through puddles. Fall was the best time for these outings, as many of the bugs had died off, and it was easy to get her hitched up without having to slap them away or saturate her with spray.

I stood with Trudy, holding her bridle while my sister Amanda climbed slowly into the cart. Amanda had Down's Syndrome, and among her other physical problems, she had been through several knee surgeries. It was important to hold the cart as still as possible.

Once Amanda was settled in, I took the reins and climbed in. "Okay, let's go!"

Like most Morgan horses, Kerry Airatude – Trudy for short -- was born to trot. Her knees and hocks flew skyward as the cart whizzed along. Her little snorts told us that she was enjoying the outing. Amanda and I laughed and sang songs. My dogs Reva and Scorch, and half-grown pup Cajun galloped along after us. All around us, autumn leaves fluttered to the ground, and the road was lined with purple asters and goldenrod.

Drummond Island was considered one of the Isles of the Manitou by Native American tribes who had lived there for centuries. To others, it was known as the Gem of the Huron. It was a jewel of green suspended in the sapphire waters between Lakes Superior and Huron, an isolated world within itself. It was a land of rock and tundra, jagged cliffs and gently rolling sandy hills. It was covered with twisted ancient cedars, pointed spruce and tall white poplar with round shivering leaves that sang in a hushed whisper of home.

I had cause to celebrate, because after four years of discomfort and dental chairs and metal tools, my braces were about to come off. I would leave Michigan's Upper Peninsula, traveling back downstate to the orthodontist and have the implements of torture permanently removed. I couldn't imagine what it would be like to finally, at age 38, have teeth that were smooth and straight, and pain-free!

Amanda and I took a long drive that day, heading down to the Drummond Island fairgrounds where the annual rodeo was held; now a bare field with bits of brown leaves rasping across the grasses. The dogs gamboled happily, tongues flopping with joy. We took a break there, so my twelve-year-old German shepherd Reva could rest. Amanda and I took pictures of each other.

Finally we decided to head back to camp. It was about two miles back, and we were rounding the last curve when I noticed that the traces on Trudy's harness were coming loose from the cart shafts.

"Whoa," I said, and she stopped immediately. But we were close to home, and she was impatient to get back. She danced a little step or two.

"Look at that," I said to Amanda, nodding toward the shafts. They were swinging, banging against the sides of the mare. I thought if I could get her to stand still, I would tell Amanda to climb out of the cart, and then I could get out afterward and fix them. Had I been by myself, I could have jumped right out. But for Amanda, climbing out of the cart was not a simple task. It was important for Trudy to stand quietly.

"Easy, Trudy," I said. But the more the shafts swung, the more she danced. I gave a little tug on the reins. "Whoa! Stand!"

The next thing I knew, I was face down on the ground. I lay flat on my stomach, listening to the rapidly diminishing hoofbeats of a galloping horse. I could feel grit and tiny stones in my mouth, and I spit them out. I lifted my head and looked back at the cart. Amanda still sat there quietly, staring at me.

"Are you okay?" I asked.

"Yes," she said calmly. "But I think you need stitches."

I felt no pain, but I knew I had broken my nose. I stood up and noticed the road was splashed with red, and there was a huge red stain on my jacket. My nose was running, pouring blood. There was a salty taste in my mouth.

"Come on," I said to Amanda. "Let's get this cart off the road."

Trudy was nowhere in sight. The dogs had gone with her. Amanda climbed out of the cart and we pulled it into the weeds. I walked up to camp and went into the trailer for a washcloth. I looked at my face in the mirror. The entire lower half of it was covered in blood. There was a huge hole between my nose and mouth. My nose looked okay, but when I looked in my mouth, I saw that my two front teeth were pushed way back inside. The braces had kept them from coming out. And my nose was bleeding. Blood was everywhere. It dripped onto the sink while I stood there. It ran all down the front of my coat. I took a washcloth, soaked it, and pressed it against my upper lip. I tried to wipe the blood from the countertop, but it was falling faster than I could wipe it up. I didn't want to leave a mess, but finally gave up. I still felt no pain.

I went back outside where Amanda stood waiting.

"Well," I said. "We'd better go get Dad."

"What about Trudy?"

"Reva will take care of her. Come on."

Dad was working with some volunteer builders, putting an addition on the Drummond Island Laundry. It was only a couple of miles down the road. When we pulled up, I said, "Amanda, would you please go tell Dad what has happened? I don't want him to be too shocked when he sees me."

Amanda climbed out. "Dad! We've had a little accident!"

Dad walked over as I got out of the truck. He hesitated when he saw me. There I stood, with that bloodied washcloth pressed against my rapidly blackening face. "The harness broke. She pulled me out by the reins."

"Oh, honey! Did you break your teeth?"

"I think so."

"I'm sorry!" He pulled me against him. I looked up and saw all the volunteers -- seven or eight men in their fifties, gaping at me.

"I guess I should go to the hospital."

"Can you drive?" Dad said. "I'll have to take my truck. I'll follow you."

"I can drive. Trudy's still out there somewhere. Could you ask Uncle Bob to go look for her? Reva's with her."

I drove the ten miles to the ferry dock, rolling onto the boat somewhat self-consciously, with my washcloth still smashed against my lip. The attendants, whom Amanda and I called the Ferry Boys, did not appear to notice. But when I walked into Mom's house, she took one look at me and burst into tears.

"Oh my God, Nancy!" she wailed.

"You should see the other guy," I quipped through the washcloth. Behind me, I heard Dad laugh.

People reacted that same shocked way for the rest of the afternoon. Entering the emergency room at the hospital, I was greeted by alarmed stares. After Mom and Dad left, there were more stares as I went in for the CAT scan. I was left alone in one exam room for a long time, after being informed that I would need surgery.

I thought of my friend Kimmy, who had suffered a head injury during an encounter with a shoplifter. Kimmy was head of security for J.C. Penney in a southern California store. She was about five foot four, had earned a black belt in karate, and harbored the kind of fury that only natural redheads comprehend. She had adopted the store as her own. She took theft very personally. Once, she had caught a six foot three "suspect" making off with a leather jacket, chased him out into the mall and after a brief scuffle, found herself flat on her back while he smashed her head repeatedly into the cement floor.

The police showed up and arrested the guy. Kim suffered a concussion, but after a brief recovery period, she went on to collar more criminals. During her long and very successful career, she had undergone a number of surgeries to correct various injuries.

I would have liked to talk to her just then, but she was in California. I had never experienced anesthesia before. I had a fleeting impulse to have someone call Cheryl Smith, my veterinarian. I wanted to ask her to come and sit in on my surgery. I thought I'd feel more secure with her there. I realized it would take her five hours to get there, and they wouldn't be willing to wait that long, even if she would come. Besides, now it was midnight. And anyway, it might offend someone. I pictured myself explaining my request to the nurse, and Cheryl driving the long road to the Upper Peninsula, in the middle of the night, to come and hold my hand. I started giggling out loud, with my clogged and bloody nose, lying alone on the gurney in the exam room.

What seemed like hours later, as I was wheeled into surgery, heads turned as I rolled past. In the operating room, the anesthesiologist even said, "We're not staring at you."

"Yes you are. Go ahead. I would."

Oddly enough, there still was no pain, although by now I had taken pills for it. I lay flat on my back and the anesthesiologist held a mask suspended above my face. "I can't put this on your nose because it's broken," he explained. "Count backwards from a hundred."

I thought I would certainly be able to count with no problem. After all, I felt completely alert and just fine, except for the odd fact that I couldn't seem to stop my eyes from rapidly blinking.

The rest of the experience was surreal. The first thing I remember was a nurse telling me, "Trudy is fine."

My intelligent response was, "Huh?"

"You were asking about her."

I knew she was fine. Reva, the matriarchal German shepherd, was taking care of her. I drifted off again and watched red dots drifting over rocks underwater.

Later, I was told that it had taken three and a half hours of surgery to irrigate the gravel from my mouth, stitch the cuts inside my mouth and nose, and prevent my crushed nose from collapsing into itself. My two front teeth had been knocked out, but were still attached to the orthodontia which I had been wearing. The surgeon had bent my braces and forced my teeth back into position, but I was going to need a lot of dental work. He was amazed that I hadn't broken my jaw. I did, however, suffer a concussion. I had been laughing hysterically and making jokes when I was coming out of the anesthesia, but I didn't remember that.

The nurse came into my room in the wee hours that morning, saying happily, "Look who's here to see you!"

Right behind her was my husband, Bruce. I was surprised. He had been working long hours, carving generous portions into the abyss that widened between us.

"What are you doing here?"

"I canceled my meeting."

When he said that, I realized that my injuries must be fairly serious. He had driven the five hours north and then sat with me in the hospital all night. He drove me back to Mom and Dad's and took care of the dogs while I languished on the couch.

That was when the pain started roaring and hammering through my head, neck and face. I had to eat through a straw. I was sick to my stomach constantly, and dropped weight immediately. My neck crackled and crunched like a bowl of Rice Krispies every time I turned my head. One of the worst parts of it was, due to the nerve damage in my nose and upper lip, I couldn't tell when my nose was running!

But I just knew that I was going to get a new nose out of the deal, and it would all be worth it.

"Rhinoplasty may be in my future!" I chirped excitedly to anyone who asked how I was doing. "Do you want to help me pick my nose?"

I was so anxious to see the horses again, but was told I absolutely could not ride. On the first day home, I asked to be taken to Drummond to see Trudy and her half-brother, Clifford. They were in the corral when we pulled up. They neighed a greeting and came to the gate. Trudy looked none the worse for wear. I went up to them, but Clifford's head swinging around my face made me nervous. I wish I could say it was a happy reunion, but I was too ill to spend any time with them. I went and sat on the grass in the sun while chickadees dive-bombed me, looking for seeds.

"This is just like in the cartoons," I thought as the birds chirped and fluttered around my head. "Now someone just needs to draw a big X over each of my eyes."

I was sick for weeks. When I finally was able to travel again, and the horses were hauled down to my farm for the winter, I was told that I'd need to spend another six months in braces, plus have two root canals and crowns on my four front teeth. I wasn't happy about it, but I realized that I was lucky. I could easily have broken my neck.

The whole experience left me wishing that I had checked and oiled the ancient harness, which had given way and caused the shafts to swing. The cart was put away and I didn't try to drive again. I waited weeks before riding again, but before getting the go-ahead, I saddled up Clifford and, swollen face and all, swung aboard. Despite his propensity for practical jokes, I knew that I could trust him. He walked in circles slowly, like an old nag, as if he was carrying eggs. That was fine with me.

I looked in the mirror every day, examining my nose, turning my head this way and that. I was hoping as the swelling went down, that the nose would be crooked or mangled or at least pocked beyond recognition. Alas, it was becoming more and more like my own old bulbous nose. I was, however, comforted by the fact that I had a year to wait before healing was considered complete. Maybe something would be a little off. Scars threaded, red and angry, above my upper lip. I was secretly nervous about those.

But the healing progressed, and even though it seemed I was spending half my life in a dental chair, the headaches dissipated. And then the jokes began. My friend Ray Benter wrote the following to an email list:

"I think Nancy was being a little nosy, don't you? Er, ahem, just a little humor there. Don't want to upset Nancy, like the American expression, we don't want her to get her 'nose out of joint!' You know, I think she'll be all well by the time we run out of these nose jokes .... but who nose!?!"

I replied, "It snot unlike Ray to sinus up for such awful puns. Ah well, it's really no skin off my nose."

But I was wrong. The trouble was only beginning.

Chapter Two

"But over all things brooding slept the quiet sense of something lost."
~ Lord Alfred Tennyson

The day after my accident, the phone rang at my parents' house. "Nancy? This is Shell."

The pit of my stomach yawned, stretching into a sickened hole. Before her next words came, I knew what she was going to say. "Patty died yesterday."

It was Piper the Papillon who had first introduced me to the dog groomer, Patty, three years prior. Patty was a pretty brunette, edging on fifty, who lived alone with her own Papillons, Buzz and L.B. Whenever I took Piper in for grooming, Patty would want to stand around and visit, sometimes for an hour. We talked a lot about dog stuff, rescue, training, and of course her favorite breed, the Papillon "butterfly" dog.

One of the things that endeared Patty to me was the way she laughed at all my jokes. She would look up with a smile when I came in, and shout my name. She made me feel like a movie star. She was always bright and cheerful, always seemed happy.

But then I got a call from my friend Rita, who had bad news. "Do you know that dog groomer, Patty? She has cancer. She has six months to live and doesn't know what she's going to do with her dogs. It's really sad."

I immediately asked Bruce if I could take Buzz and L.B. as a foster parent. To his credit, he agreed.

I didn't know how to approach Patty about it, though. We were friendly, but not really that close. Finally one day, I walked into the shop and said, "Patty, I hear you're having a bit of a dilemma about Buzzy and L.B. I'd be happy to help out if you need a place for them to stay."

"You would, really? That would be wonderful!"

Her welcoming smile encouraged me to go a step further. "So you have cancer? What kind?"

To my surprise, she was eager to talk about it. "I have ovarian cancer. I would have been okay if they had diagnosed me earlier."

She went on for awhile, describing the tests and doctors and more tests and doctors, and how tiresome that was. I began to wonder if she has anyone else to talk to. On that day, I decided to be an open vessel for Patty. I would be her ear.

As I walked out of the shop, I was thinking, "I don't know her that well, so she won't need to worry about the damage it might do to me, hearing of her pain. I am just distant enough to be useful to her."

I took a part time job in the grooming shop. It was only three days a week.

"What the heck," I thought. "I'm not working. This will give Patty a chance to know me a little bit better, so she can feel more comfortable about where Buzz and L.B. go. And then we can talk. I can listen. We can talk about cancer, or whatever she feels like."

The grooming shop was a humid place, the tile floor littered with clumps of dog hair. The atmosphere was jocular and festive. David, the shop's owner, was a funny and soft hearted man that I immediately hit it off with. Patty would stand over her table, scissors in hand, and laugh as the two of us sang show tunes and told jokes.

As the weeks passed, I realized that there was so much pressure on Patty to be brave. People would come in; employees from the hospital next door, or clients from outside, and give her pitying smiles and tell her to "keep your chin up." Why couldn't people just let her be angry? Why didn't they let her cry? God knows, if I were fifty-two years old, and dying, I would want to break things. She amazed me. She was so concerned about others. She didn't want to be a burden to anyone. She almost carried it too far. I wished I could do more.

As more time passed, I marveled at how tough she was. She was starting to move more slowly. Her hair fell out, due to the chemotherapy, and she had to wear wigs. She told me that sometimes she felt pain. She could feel the tumor pressing in certain areas.

I thought of the TV movies about people dying of cancer and how brave and inspirational they were. Well, real life isn't like that. It is ugly. It robs people of their strength and pallor. There was nothing beautiful about watching my friend die. She was scared and angry.

Patty lived a year and a half after her diagnosis. She worked for most of that time. She and I discussed what was best for Buzz and L.B., and we decided that she would keep them with her as long as possible, and then I would find them a home after she died.

"I really want them to stay together," she said. "They're very bonded."

"They will. I promise."

She paused. "I just don't want everyone to forget me. I'm afraid they will."

I was brushing a Shih Tzu at the time. I dragged the slicker through the dog's long hair thoughtfully, stopping to break a tangle apart with my fingers.

"Well, Patty," I said. "I won't forget you. I've known few people with your kind of moxie."

She snorted a little. "Yeah, right."

"I can't imagine what it's like to be in your position. But I think this might be an opportunity to come up with some really quotable thing. You know, some grand statement that people will repeat after you are gone. They're really listening to you right now! It's the ordinary people that folks forget."

She said nothing, but a little smile played about her lips. I realized later that she appreciated my effort, but I just wasn't getting it.

Finally, Patty was hospitalized. Buzzy and L.B. came home with me. On the first day I went to visit her, I took L.B. with me. Patty looked up and smiled from her hospital bed and called my name.

When I got home that night, I suddenly felt weak in the knees. I had to sit down on the front porch. I was bent over, shaken. I realized that I had made a big mistake in thinking I could remain "distant" from Patty, a sort of impartial and supportive ear. I was swept into it all, now immersed tossed and scrambling down the rushing canal shared by those who love the terminally ill.

The tears began to flood down my face, and I struggled to breathe. To my embarrassment, Bruce arrived home from work just then, and found me.

He stood beside me, looking down. "What's the matter? Are you sick? Has something happened?"

"Yes. No. I'm just surprised."

"Surprised?"

"I went into this trying to help someone. I didn't know this would be so hard. I didn't know the world was losing one of its truly kind and generous people. I thought I could do something about this. I can't!"

Bruce stood there, helplessly, and I finally got up and went into the house.

Now Patty was gone and I found myself explaining to Shell that I'd had an accident, I couldn't travel yet and I would have to miss the funeral.

Weeks later, I walked into the animal hospital's boarding room and there in one of the cages stood Buzz, the red sable with big brown eyes like dark glass baubles, and L.B. with his long ear fringe, soft black curtains framing his face. They wagged and danced at the sight of me.

As I lifted them out of the cage, I felt their delicate bones beneath the velvet skin, their plumed tails stirring the air, their claws pushing against me as they stretched and struggled to lick my face in greeting. I had a flashback to Patty, standing over her table, looking up with a radiant smile and calling my name. I wished I had told her that she hadn't had to leave anything, to say anything special. For someone like Patty, to be was memorable enough.

Chapter Three

*"I'm Nobody! Who are you?
Are you Nobody, too?"
~ Emily Dickinson*

Reva stood quietly on the examining table, but her legs trembled slightly. She didn't like standing up there. The smooth cold surface must have felt slippery and dangerous. And there was the gentle but impersonal groping of Doctor Anne Hale, feeling her abdomen. It was a routine exam. Reva was twelve and a half years old, suffering with – or rather dealing with – arthritis and hip dysplasia. She had been on a drug called Rimadyl which helped with the stiffness and pain in her joints. Rimadyl was known to be hard on the liver, so I wanted to make sure she was okay.

But then Anne used the expression every pet owner dreads: "Uh oh. What's this?"

She palpated Reva's abdomen. I clenched my teeth, then quickly unclenched them as they shrieked a silent protest. It was only a month after my accident.

"A tumor." Anne leaned back and looked at the dog. Reva rolled a worried eye back at her. "It's on her spleen. You're not gonna like me for saying this, but there are a hundred other things I'd rather see."

In fact, I wasn't happy hearing this news. I was pretty sure that Reva's sire, a beautiful male shepherd imported from Germany, had died from this very thing at age ten.

"Well, we'll have Cheryl take it out first thing tomorrow. These things tend to bleed, and that's what makes them so dangerous. If there are cancer cells, that's how they'll spread."

I was immediately relieved to hear Cheryl was going to be involved. She was a humane and gifted surgeon. I viewed her with the adoration the public had seen in Joe Dimaggio or Charles Lindbergh: She was my hero.

Anne's speech took an optimistic turn. "We're very lucky to catch it this early. This kind of tumor is usually not discovered until it bleeds out. And Reva is strong -- she has great muscle tone for a dog her age."

I brightened. Reva had been eating well, and appeared to be completely normal. But something had told me she needed to see the vet. I had called that morning and Anne had seen her the same day. I felt someone was looking out for us.

The next day I stood in the operating room and watched as Cheryl's doll-sized hands reached into my precious dog and pulled out a tumor the size of a tennis ball.

"It's well contained," Cheryl said through her mask. She tossed the tumor into a plastic bin. "We'll get the biopsy right out and have samples in a few days. But we'll have to test her again in six months. This type of tumor is typical of lymphoma."

Her deft fingers moved around the dog's insides. The rib cage rose and fell steadily as Reva breathed. Her heart thumped vigorously. "It all looks good in here," Cheryl said. "I see you had her tattooed with an ID number."

"Yeah, all my dogs are."

"Whoever tattooed her put it right over her navel. That's right where a surgeon makes the incision. That's a dumb place for a tattoo. Who did that?"

"You did! Eight years ago!"

She grinned and shook her head. I started laughing.

I went home for lunch when Reva started to wake up. Cheryl called later and said I could bring her home that night. "Just keep an eye on her. You'll know if anything's not right."

She was correct, as usual. Reva was peaceful and happy to be home, but she needed to urinate, a lot. She kept going to the door. I was suddenly relating to her condition. I thought it must have something to do with the anesthesia, because I remembered when I was in the hospital how I had to keep ringing the nurse to come and take me to the bathroom! I didn't fret about her lack of appetite, either, because I remembered how that was too. And out of courtesy, I didn't touch her anywhere near her incision. People touching my face and nose had made me so nervous. All I had wanted to do was sleep, and that is what Reva did now.

That night, Bruce came home from a business trip to find me pacifying myself with chocolate ice cream. He walked in the door with briefcase in hand, set it down, and said hello.

"Reva's had surgery." I nodded to where she lay by my feet. "She may have cancer."

It was the big ugly word again, and here we were just fresh from Patty's experience. But Bruce barely looked at Reva.

Then he used the expression that every spouse dreads: "I need to talk to you."

"Uh oh," I joked.

His eyes snapped. He was clearly in a bad mood. "I want you to start having dinner ready for me when I get home!"

My intelligent response was, "Huh?"

"You don't cook for me!"

"Sure I do! I do at least half of the cooking."

"Then where's my dinner? And you don't clean this house!" His gestured toward the kitchen table, cluttered with art supplies from my latest project.

I felt completely ambushed. I just sat there. I couldn't understand where all this sudden aggression was coming from. There had been a distance between us, which had grown over the years, and it was often difficult to get two words out of Bruce. Now he was suddenly exploding with hostility.

"You're not a wife! What are you?"

I couldn't answer.

He continued, "I'm an engineer! You're a Nothing!"

When he said the word, "Nothing", he bent forward and flung out his arms in the exact gesture an umpire would use when yelling, "Safe!" A little breeze puffed across my bangs as his hand flew past my face. *Whiff*, it said.

My face felt hot. I couldn't look at him. I hesitated, then got up and left the room, and sat down on the stairs. I realized that this moment marked a turning point in the marriage, and maybe in my life. Though my heart was banging in my chest, my thoughts were whirling philosophy. What makes a person valuable? Is it what you do, or who you are, that matters most? Or does one lend validity to the other? I knew I had basically flunked as a wife. I couldn't even label myself. What was I? Helper of dying friends? Caring dog owner? And now with my scarred face and swollen nose and broken teeth, I was sure no beauty queen.

After a few moments I realized I was weeping, and it was a horrible experience. I couldn't breathe. All the scar tissue in my nose was throbbing, and my nose was running like never before. I needed a tissue – or maybe a whole box of them. Reva, though heavy with sleep and aching from the incision, heaved herself to her feet. She walked over to me and shoved her big, furry head under my arm, forcing me into that familiar embrace, and began to lick my cheek.

I looked at her. There she sat, panting a little, anxious. She wasn't worried about her own pain. She was worried about mine. I patted her and thought, well, maybe I could learn by example. Maybe I should go ask Bruce if he'd had a rough week, or whatever.

But I couldn't do it. I recoiled at the thought of facing more criticism.

I looked at Reva. "You're a better man than I am."

She sighed and rested her head on my knee, content to just be a Loyal Dog. I envied her.

I wasn't a Kimmy or a Patty, or even a Reva for that matter. But I knew I had to be made of tougher stuff than this.

Chapter Four

"No problem can withstand the assault of sustained thinking."
~ Voltaire

As nine-year-old Blaine Bailey crawled out his bedroom window and scooted down the back porch roof, he remembered his mother's admonitions that morning to not go skating on the river ice.

"It hasn't been cold enough this year," she said.

It seemed plenty cold that day. He blew misty puffs into the brittle air as the snow squeaked beneath his feet. The Saint Mary's River beckoned him. It was Christmas vacation, 1934, and freedom from school shouldn't be wasted.

"Besides," he thought, giving a tug on the string of his Flyer wooden snow sled, "She never said I couldn't go sledding."

Blaine wandered down the hill, watching for any traitorous adult spies who might happen past. He was a short, wiry boy with wide, sloping shoulders and sturdy legs. It was a small town and he would surely be recognized even bundled up as he was.

Below him was an expanse of smooth, inviting river ice. He pulled the sled up beside him and sat on it while he removed the red woolen mittens his mother had knitted. They were a Christmas gift, warm and rough and new-smelling.

He tied his boot laces and then flung himself belly-down on the sled. In minutes he was gliding out on the ice, gazing down at the cracks and bubbles and the black water beneath him. He looked out across the river at Drummond Island a mile away, and thought longingly about his summer home on the farm. Village life wasn't the same, but at least he had a nice place to sled.

He skidded to a stop, grabbed the string and tugged his sled back up the hill. This time he took a running start, carrying the sled, and threw himself across it as it flew toward the river. He grabbed the handle, and steered himself this way and that as he bumped along, giddily withholding any shrieks of delight for fear of being discovered.

As he hurtled farther and farther out on the ice, his sled topped a ledge that had been forced up by the current. He was airborne for a moment, and then boy and sled plopped softly down with a soft splash.

The next thing he knew, he was under water. He couldn't remember taking a deep breath, but his lungs were full of air, his lips pressed tightly together. The cold scissored through him. Below him was a gravel bed, sand and gray rocks. He looked up and saw a light spot in the ceiling of ice above him.

A powerful boy for his age, he was already a strong swimmer. He reached up to put a hand through the opening. To his surprise, his mitten hit solid ice. It was not the hole he had fallen through, after all.

His eyes scanned the surface above him. Several feet away was a dark spot. He swam toward it, and his head burst up through the water. He gasped for air, but then realized he had forgotten his sled. He took another breath and looked down, to see it peacefully resting on the bottom. He swam down and grabbed it, and carried it up with him.

The moment he pushed that sled through the hole, and watched it glide beyond his reach, he knew he had made a mistake. He could have perhaps used it as a brace or a prop somehow to pull himself out. Now, he gasped for air as he flung his arms up onto the ice.

His teeth rattled with the cold. He looked around, but could see no one on the shore's white hillside.

"Help!" he roared.

There was silence.

He called again, but received no answer.

As he was suspended there, it occurred to him that he had better keep moving, to ward off frostbite. He kicked his feet, but could no longer feel his toes. He raised his arm, and his woolen mitten peeled off the ice with an adhesive rip. Startled, he looked at the other hand. He wiggled his stiffening fingers and realized that mitten had stuck, too.

A revelation came to him. He stretched both arms up across the ice, as far as he could, and pressed his mittens against the cold surface. He waited. He began to shiver convulsively, but patiently held his hands motionless.

Finally, he edged his hands backward. The wet mittens remained there, frozen firmly to the lake ice. He grabbed them, and with a mighty pull, hauled himself up.

He staggered to his feet. He forced himself to move quickly, grabbing the sled's string as he passed it.

When he reached the top of the hill, he looked back out over the river. There, by the hole in the ice, were two bright spots that were his mittens.

Chapter Five

"Every investigation which is guided by principles of nature fixes its ultimate aim entirely on gratifying the stomach."
~ Cooks' and Confectioners' Dictionary

"You want to do more cooking to save your marriage?" Kimmy's voice crackled over the phone. "That won't work. Look at me. I cooked all the time for Gary. In fact, I still cook for him."

"What?" I screeched.

"Sure. I cook for him and his new wife. I send dinner over there every time Makayla goes back."

"Well, I could understand you making dinner for Makayla, of course, since she is your daughter, but feeding Gary's new wife? Now, that's a little above and beyond!"

Her evil laugh told me something else was going on.

"Kimmy. What are you up to?"

"I make two versions of everything. I use real butter in their food, low fat margarine in mine. I use whole milk in anything I bake for them. I've been sending a lot of French fries this month."

"What on earth…"

"You should see them!" she cackled triumphantly. "Their clothes don't fit anymore! By summer, they're both gonna weigh over three hundred pounds!"

I crowed, "Talk about moxie!"

"Moxie, what exactly is that?"

"Facing challenges with spirit and courage. And, I think, pizzazz. You've got that."

I was making a green bean casserole. We had many beans from the garden, frozen, about 14 quarts of them. Those bean plants just kept growing beans and more beans. I ate raw green beans, boiled green beans and took green beans up north. I gave beans to all my friends, and still there were more beans.

That day, I thought I'd put them in a bowl with some mushroom soup, and put them in the oven. It seemed simple enough.

I preheated the oven. I hung up the phone, and put the beans in a bowl. They were easy to snap, being frozen and all. So I broke them up into small bean pieces. I opened up a can of mushrooms, congratulating myself on my culinary instincts.

Then the smoke alarm went off. I looked, and there was smoke rolling out of the top of the oven. I opened the oven door. With a gentle "poof", the flames erupted.

My oven was burning, no doubt consuming the grease from the Christmas turkey that Bruce had cooked.

I slammed the door shut and ran to turn off the smoke alarm. I couldn't stand that shrieking noise it made. Then I opened the windows. The dogs milled about in alarm.

"Settle down!" I shouted. "Have faith in me!"

Smoke was filling the house. Cajun began to whimper. I opened the oven door again, and the flames leaped higher. I shut the door and rummaged through the cupboard for a box of cornstarch. I found half a box, opened the oven, and flung the remains onto the fire. It died down a little.

I rummaged again and found a new box of cornstarch. I ripped it open and poured half of it on the flames. I shut the door. There was cornstarch all over the counter and floors, and all over me.

Bruce came in then. "What's going on in here?"

"There was a fire, but I have it all under control."

"Cornstarch? You're supposed to use baking soda!" He ran to the kitchen. "Get back!" he shouted to the worried dogs, who were clustering around him. He looked into the oven. "It's burning the cornstarch."

The house was getting cold, because the windows were still open. The various smoke alarms continued to screech. Finally, the fire died and I opened the oven door to reveal a blackened, charred, smoking mess inside.

When I told Kimmy about it later, she said, "Next time, just deep fry his beans."

Chapter Six

"Gitchee Manitou became so angered by the way Man treated the animals that he drew a huge crack in the ground separating them. Man stood on one side watching the crack grow deeper and wider, and the animals getting farther out of reach. Finally at the last moment,
Dog jumped over the crack to join Man, where he remained at his side forever."
~ Native American Legend

"With affection beaming in one eye, and calculation shining out of the other."

-- Charles Dickens

"Scorch, are you there?" said the voice on my answering machine. "Scorch! Pick up the phone!"

It was my brother Ted, calling from Arizona. He always left messages for my dog Scorch. He was convinced that at some point, Scorch would pick up the phone and talk to him.

Scorch was half Australian shepherd, a rescued mutt who was originally intended to be a temporary foster pup. How he came to me was in a predestined way similar to what Trudy had. However, in Scorch's case, it was very clearly the animal's choice.

Many of the foster homes didn't appreciate puppies. They were notoriously messy and noisy at night. The work involved in raising a puppy was intimidating to even the most avid of dog lovers. But I had it down to a science. I had my own effective methods for crate training and obedience training. I employed the use of Operant Conditioning, better known as the clicker method, a technique invented by dolphin trainers. It was now catching on in the dog fancy. A small plastic noise maker signaled "yes" to the animal when the desired behavior occurred. I had used the clicker on all my dogs and the horses too. It was a most humane and scientific method.

Puppies were cute, but the thing I liked best about them was watching the "light bulb" go on. I had become so entranced with the process of learning that I found myself perpetually fostering homeless puppies. Bruce had regulated me to one foster at a time. Otherwise things might have gotten out of hand, since an endless barrage of homeless puppies seemed to flood my existence.

My current foster pup at that time was a sort of Golden Retriever in miniature, complete with a distinctive black mask. She was a very cute, mild-mannered little thing, whom I had dubbed Ursa Minor, meaning "Little Bear". I had taken her to an Adopt-a-Pet day at a grooming shop in Ann Arbor. As the afternoon wore on, potential adopters straggled in and out. I interviewed some, but no one was striking me quite right as a potential home for Ursa.

I had immediately noticed a pair of Australian shepherd mix puppies lying by the back wall. They were about twelve weeks old. The male was darker, mostly black with some merling on his face. The female was gray, with longer hair and more lovely merle and tan markings. They huddled together, watching the proceedings with gentle passivity. I had been told that they had come from a litter of eight, which were turned in with their mother to the dog pound in Jackson. The rescue group had acquired the entire batch and these two remained.

I was drawn to herding dogs and admired both pups. They were lovely, and so calm, despite the fact that they were obviously over stimulated by the goings-on. The female was the prettier of the two. But the male had round, dark eyes that bored right into mine. As the afternoon wore on, the two continued to lie there unmoving. Every time I looked at the boy dog, he was staring right back at me.

Ursa Minor greeted people happily as I chatted with them, but I couldn't get past the feeling that I was being watched. I would often turn during conversation to see the Aussie puppy staring at me. His expression was knowing and warm, although he did not move, nor did he even raise his head from where it rested on the floor.

Finally the shadows lengthened and Adoption Day was drawing to a close. Thankfully, several dogs found homes that day. However, neither Aussie pup was adopted. Ursa Minor, due in part to my particularly over-zealous screening techniques, was not adopted out either.

"Well, that's the way it goes!" I cheerfully stood up and paused by the door, holding the end of Ursa's leash. "I'd better get home. I guess I'll see you guys la-"

I stopped because I had seen movement from the quiet ones in the corner. Rising from the spot where he had stayed all day long, the dark Aussie male stood up and daintily approached me. He carefully placed his tiny front feet, which where tan and marbled with black, up on the front of my jacket. He stood there on his hind legs, calmly looking up into my face.

"Uh oh," I said.

His message was unmistakable. The other rescue people started laughing. "Nancy's taking another dog home!" they crowed.

I did take the Aussie pup home. Unfortunately, Bruce was not happy about this in the least. He took one look at the little black dog and said, "You need to send him back to Joann's, right now. I've told you, only one foster dog at a time."

"But, you don't understand. This dog chose me."

"Then send Ursa. Although you've had her nearly a year and I don't think that would be a very nice thing to do. But you're going to have to take your pick. Besides, that is an ugly dog anyway."

I looked at the Aussie pup who stood quietly by my side. He was still searching my face with the dignified expression of an elderly gentleman. He was a little unconventional, but I didn't think him ugly at all. He was very fine-boned and had strange shades of ashy gray on his face and belly and sides. The rest of him was burnt black, except for his reddish tan legs and feet, which were freckled with black spots. Most endearing of all was his extreme head tilt whenever I spoke to him. He would look up at me, ears perked, head tipping to one side and then the other. He appeared to be listening intently, digesting my every word.

Reluctantly, I realized that I had to prioritize my marriage.

"Fine. I'll call Joann."

I called her and she agreed to come and get the puppy. Meanwhile, I decided to see how the pup would respond to my training method. I was a clicker trainer. It was a Pavlovian form of training originating with people who worked with dolphins. They couldn't put a leash on a dolphin, so they had to learn another way to teach them. Dolphin trainers used a whistle, but for dogs they had adapted this to a clicker, a small plastic noisemaker that made a popping sound when it was squeezed. The click said "yes" to the animal, and told them food was coming. The idea was to click at the moment the desired behavior was occurring. It communicated very clearly to a dog. Besides that, it was fun. I used it on my horses too.

I got out some hot dog pieces and the little dog quickly comprehended the message of the click. Within minutes he had learned to "Sit" on a hand signal.

"Look at this!" I shrieked. "Look how smart he is!"

The little dog sat promptly, head tilting this way and that, eager to learn the next thing. His expression glowed with intelligence. After working with him for several minutes, I understood even more deeply that this dog was very special.

I grudgingly sent him home with Joann. Several weeks went by, and I thought of him from time to time, but decided I would probably never see him again. Meanwhile, I had a stroke of luck with Ursa Minor – I found her a home with a good friend of mine who was looking for a companion for her Border Collie.

So when I walked into the animal hospital one day, I was sans puppies. Jane Price, the receptionist, greeted me. "Hey Nancy! How have you been?"

"Jest dandy."

"Hey, there's a little dog in the back that you should see. It's one of Joann's rescue puppies. He has a broken foot."

I was overcome with an eerie chill. It was not particularly odd that Jane would mention this to me, but I somehow knew which puppy it was. I went back into the ward, and sure enough, there in the cage was my little friend. He again regarded me with that kindly intense expression. His left front paw was consumed by a huge cast.

"How did you do that?" I asked. His head cranked to one side. I laughed, opened the door and took him out. When I put him on the floor, he promptly sat – plop – directly in front of me.

"You remember me!" I gasped. I picked him up and carried him back through the lobby. "Jane, I'm taking this dog home."

She waved, and we were off.

Bruce's face clouded when I walked in the front door carrying the Aussie. "You are not keeping that dog."

"I'm going to raise him for a year and then donate him to Paws with a Cause," I announced.

Paws with a Cause was a group that trained service and hearing ear dogs. The group was careful about matching dogs with owners, and I especially liked the fact that they used the clicker method.

I decided to name the puppy Scorch, due to his charred black and ashy gray coat. The name fit also because of the way his eyes snapped with brilliance.

I didn't know how he had broken his foot, but he was very nervous about doorways, stairways, tile floors or any smooth surface. He would brace himself, all four legs wooden, and freeze, stiff and unmoving.

I decided that an agility class was the ticket, where he would have to climb over and through various obstacles. It did help, and it helped that the dog loved to learn. He was like an honor student who tackled each course with relish and looked forward to the next challenge. Scorch turned out to have a penchant for the clicker, and was hungry to learn everything.

He had a sort of charisma that attracted people to him. Even Reva was uncharacteristically patient with him, probably due to his innocuous nature. Though he was friendly and cuddly with everyone, he never lost that strange and immediate bond to me. He watched my every move. If I got up and left the room, he would immediately follow and station himself in a place where he could see me.

It wasn't long before I realized that there was no way I was ever going to be able to part with this gentle and intelligent creature. So, in order to get Bruce to warm up to him, I began teaching him a multitude of tricks, which he learned with great enthusiasm. Everyone who came to the house was witness to the latest thing. He would grin, baring all his teeth, on cue. The crowd favorite was when he "said his prayers" – putting his paws up on a chair and hiding his face in them. People also loved, "Bless You", when he would pull a piece of tissue from the box when I sneezed. But my great accomplishment was when he learned to walk on three legs as if wounded. He began to receive invitations to parties and once he even performed on stage during our community theatre's production of, "Joseph and the Amazing Technicolor Dreamcoat."

Over the years, Scorch's repertoire grew to the point of almost being ridiculous. He knew so much stuff even I couldn't remember it all. But it worked. His place was enshrined in the family due to the tricks, and Bruce never forced me to place him.

The Native Americans believed when a dog was your spirit helper, you were protected, and were constantly surrounded by loyalty, love and true devotion. Scorch was the epitome of this. He remained my constant companion, and was a great comfort to me through my recovery from the accident, and the subsequent things that happened. To this day I wonder how I ever got so lucky.

He never did answer the phone, but I don't either. After all, that's what the machine is for.

Chapter Seven

"Faith is love taking the form of aspiration."
~ William Ellery Channing

My friend Jennifer adored my dogs, but horses were another matter. She had always liked Zach the Rescue Morgan though. He had had a bit of a rough start, and she liked to root for the underdog. Zach was very sweet, cuddly and submissive. He loved to be petted and hugged. To my surprise, Jennifer once said she would like to try riding him. I knew she'd been on horses only a few times in her life.

"Believe me," I had said. "You'd be better off riding Clifford."

It was a beautiful spring day in southern Michigan and I thought that afternoon would be a good time for her to try riding a horse. Jennifer was a person who exuded energy, and I could tell right away that Clifford was intrigued by her. He watched her as I put his halter on, eyed her as I led him out of the stall. He had been rolling in the shavings, and while I brushed him off, Jennifer regarded him with suspicion. "He's glaring at me. Why is he doing that with his mouth?"

"He's chewing. It's a sign of submission." It came out sounding like a lie.

"That's a lie! He's fantasizing about having me for dinner!"

Clifford leered and thumped his lips and swung his head. "What! What is that!" she said. "He's going to bite me! He wants to bite me!"

"That's just Clifford. That's what he does."

She leaned forward and, with a mighty gasp, blew what compared to a hurricane force wind into his face. I tried to smother a laugh, but failed.

"What!" she shrieked. "That's what you told me to do to make friends!"

"I sure did."

She bent to look down at his feet, and as the top of her head loomed closer, Clifford reached out and grabbed a strand of hair and tugged it gently forward. He let go as she straightened.

"He bit me!" she shrieked.

Clifford's eyes rolled skyward and I finally couldn't contain my laughter any more. I collapsed against him, heaving guffaws and holding my stomach while tears coursed down my cheeks.

"I KNEW it!" she roared. "This whole thing is just so you can mock me! I'm glad you're having fun."

I could not answer, by now weeping into the horse's mane. Clifford arched his neck, obviously flattered by my reaction. He pawed the ground twice with his front foot.

"Why is he doing this?" Jennifer pawed the ground with her foot, which cued him to do it more.

"Stop it!" I pleaded, sniffing and wiping my eyes. "You're just egging him on! I am never going to get him tacked up at this rate."

"But look at the way he's looking at me!" she protested. "He's looking at me balefully."

He was indeed watching her with interest, ears perked forward.

"He likes you," I said. "He pulled your hair because he likes you. He's just playing with you."

She snorted. "Sure!"

But she watched my every move while I tacked him, asking questions. "Isn't that saddle heavy? Why are you pulling that so tight? Can he breathe?"

I was surprised when she finally climbed on with no hesitation while I held one stirrup. I'd left the halter on him with a longe line, and after she was quite comfortable sitting still, I said, "Okay, I'll ask him to step forward now, so you can get the feel of him."

"You'll ASK him?"

"Yes." And I thought by that, she understood that this was a partnership, not a master/slave relationship.

He did step forward on the longe, quietly, and I could tell he was in, "Okay, Pony Ride" mode. His head was down, his eyes almost sleepy.

She smiled and waved. I was impressed with her bravery. Finally I asked if she wanted to try steering, and I said I would follow her. She learned how to go right, left, forward and stop. So I trotted around after her, holding the longe, while she rode Clifford around the yard, and pretty soon she was riding around the yard without me, and then she was asking to go around the house on her own. I did follow at a distance, just in case. And Reva and Scorch and Cajun gave her a Dog Escort.

She came back and just sat on Clifford for a long time talking and laughing and patting him, and when she finally got off, she crowed, "HE DIDN'T KILL ME!"

She stood with him in the barn aisle while I untacked him and she began scratching his face, and I warned, "He'll rub. He rubs really hard."

But she said it was okay, and in fact she let him rub his face all over her, and only laughed when he nearly pushed her over. When Clifford was finally put away, Jennifer gave him a scoop of grain.

When we came back into the house for a drink, I asked her again about her history with horses. "You have ridden more than three times, haven't you?"

"No, that was it." She explained that both times she had ridden as an adult, it was at riding stables where both horses had tried to bite her. She was never a horse lover as some kids are. Her experience as an eight-year-old was enough to warrant therapy. "I was riding this horse and he was running to the barn, and I thought he might put me through the wire fence because he was heading straight for it. And people were yelling at me to jump, so I did jump, but my foot got caught in the reins and I was dragged about a half mile. I dislocated my knee."

I looked at her. "Good grief! Why in the heck, after all that, did you ever want to ride today?"

She shrugged, took another sip of diet cola, and said, "It was Clifford, and you said it would be okay."

Chapter Eight

"Love knows not its own depth until the hour of separation."
~ Kahlil Gibran

Rumor had it that a mountain lion had been spotted on Drummond that summer. The island was rife with wild animals, including bobcats and an occasional Canadian lynx. But a cougar? It was doubtful. However, it was just plausible enough to keep me from leaving my horses corralled in the woods when I couldn't be there to supervise them. I called my cousin Tess, who had a farm with a big barn and long, flat pasture, and she said I could bring them over.

July had arrived, and with it another trip to the Upper Peninsula with the horse trailer. I was relieved and happy to be getting away from the doctors and dentists who were constantly poking and prodding at my mouth and nose. To add to the root canals and additional orthodontia, I was having colossal headaches, the like of which I had never experienced.

I left the horses for two weeks with Tess and Allen. When I came back up, I found that Trudy had fallen quite madly in love with L.T., Allen's big Arabian gelding. Clifford was still on the outskirts of the group, grazing nervously and bolting when one of the others decided to chase him. But Trudy was welcomed into the herd with the flourish bestowed upon royalty.

"L.T.'s going to miss her," Allen said, nodding toward the gelding. L.T. stood with his ears at half-mast, gazing contentedly at Trudy like a smitten teenager. He shadowed her every step and pinned his ears at other horses who ventured near.

I shook my head and smiled. "That's a shame. We're going back to camp. I want to ride down to Clifford's Bay tonight."

Trudy as always loaded into the trailer with no problem. L.T. squealed and bucked along the fence line as we pulled out and headed down the road. Trudy answered plaintively from her inside, but we were off.

After the horses were unloaded, Clifford dropped and rolled immediately in the corral, as if to say he was glad to be back. But Trudy stood in the corner, gazing wistfully down the road. I was getting the tack out, and after Clifford had stretched and rested for a minute, I put the English pad and battered old Stubben trail saddle on him.

Reva hovered eagerly nearby, watching as I buckled Clifford's bridle. Reva loved both horses, but Clifford was her special charge. She had never bonded with Trudy the same way.

I led Clifford over and opened the gate. Trudy stood inside, still looking over the fence. I swung aboard. "Come on, Airatude."

We turned and trotted up the road. Reva and Cajun whined with excitement and Scorch skipped along ahead. The poplar leaves shimmered gently in the soft clean air, and the sweet scent of balsam drifted along the dusty road. Flashes of bright orange tiger lilies lined the grassy roadside, accenting wild bouquets with the more prolific daisies.

My grandfather's old sawmill hunkered like a big gray dinosaur surrounded by birch trees and grasses and stacks of seemingly forgotten logs.

I looked back to see Trudy suddenly charging out after us as we climbed a gentle hill near the mill. Just as abruptly, she stopped, looked back, and trotted down the road with her nose in the air.

"Trudy!"

She turned.

I urged Clifford into a trot, moving swiftly away from her to encourage her to come along with us. The dogs ran along joyfully. Trudy came barreling up the road, her hoofs pounding, ta-da-DUMP ta-da-DUMP ta-da-DUMP, but then she turned back again and trotted away with determination. She let out a deep, resounding neigh that echoed through the trees.

"Good grief!" I turned back. Trudy stood in the road, clearly stymied.

I got down, walked over to her and grabbed her halter. I led her over to Clifford and she stood there while I took his bridle off and put it on her. Then I took off his saddle and saddled her up, and climbed on.

Clifford was happy to be liberated and immediately began sampling the roadside grass. Once Trudy was back under saddle, she was fine, and even seemed a little relieved. She couldn't be worried about her boyfriend now; she had to work. I thought maybe I could learn from this.

We ambled down the road, heading toward our beautiful beach, where surely the problems of our various relationships wouldn't burden any of us. However, I couldn't resist giving her a little lecture in the meantime.

"Trudy, L.T. does not stand for 'Long Term'!"

We rode on. The road to Clifford's Bay was a crooked, rock-riddled two-track. Now astride the much smoother-gaited Trudy, I was tempted to do more trotting, but went slowly so that Reva could keep up with ease. She was thirteen that year, but still loved to go on the rides. We still went every day, but had stopped doing long distance rides. It was two miles to Clifford's Bay, and Reva walked the entire way every evening with a big grin, her hips wobbling, hind toes dragging in the sand a little.

This evening she stayed with Clifford as he frisked along the trail. It was her self-appointed job to keep him out of trouble. The other dogs scampered ahead, sniffing and panting and charging after squirrels, but Reva just watched Clifford, shadowing his every move.

We rode on the beach, and the dogs swam as we crossed the bay. Gulls screamed in the distance. It was quiet on the shore, with the sun dipping into a pale sky below the tree line.

On the way back, Clifford trotted ahead and I knew he was going to ambush us again. There was a certain spot where the road split into a triangle. He took the left fork and lurked in the woods, watching like a predator as we rounded the bend. I could see his orange hide, and the white stripe on his face, held low as he peered through the brush. As Trudy and I started up the road, he snorted and charged like a furious bull, eyes rolling wildly, head flinging, mane flying as he blasted toward us at full "ramming" speed.

"Damn you!" I screeched, as he blew past, and Trudy jumped backward. It scared me every time.

He trotted in a big circle, proudly shaking his head.

As my heart slowed back to its normal pace, I said to Trudy, "See? Boys and their tricks! Who needs them?"

We walked calmly up through the little hardwood, a thick stand of fresh maple, where I had to duck my head beneath the young leaves forming a canopy over the road. As we passed, I thought of the trees and how comforting and permanent these woods were. Times change, people change and winter comes, but the great primeval forests still offered shelter, still lived on through the ages.

Chapter Nine

"The best way out is always through."
~ Robert Frost

"I saw one of your deer yesterday," I told my friend Bob. He was driving a big dump truck for the road commission that day, but had pulled over for a few minutes to chat.

"Did she have white feet?" he asked.

I couldn't remember. He had been feeding several of them at his house, which was just down the road from our camp. One of them had become quite tame and would eat out of his hand.

"Did you ever give her a name?" I asked.

He shook his head. "If I named her she'd be doomed. The hunters always shoot the ones I name."

The next day the little doe was grazing by the road. I had some horse treats in my pocket, cookies made of molasses and grain. I pulled over, got out of my truck and spoke to her. She looked up at me but did not approach. She stood still, turning her head and twisting her long ears this way and that.

Some Native American tribes believed the deer to be an intermediary between the Great Mystery and humankind. Deer could increase one's power of intuition, and increase the desire for silence and peace. The deer was considered Lord of the Dreams, purported to bring prophecies during sleep, which could be shared for the good of tribes and families.

Whitetails are possibly the loveliest of North American varieties, especially in the summer months when their coats turn a spectacular shade of warm red. But this doe was especially beautiful. She had the liquid dark eyes, long lashes and her face was masked in delicate gray. I looked down at her small cloven hoofs, and sure enough, the hair above them was white.

I noted with interest that she had a long scar on her left side, a sign that she had been struck and wounded by an arrow. I marveled that she remained so trusting.

Deer hunting was a popular sport on Drummond Island. Many people traveled from downstate to hunting camps long established, stopping along the way to buy corn and apples to use as bait.

I remembered a story told by my cousin, Bubba Bailey. He was a tower of sinew and muscle, standing six feet four inches tall and with forearms like tree limbs. He was one of the locals on Drummond Island who welcomed deer season every fall. Scorning the use of bait piles, Bubba embraced traditional hunting methods like his grandfather before him. Every animal he killed helped to feed the family that winter. He would prowl around the cliffs of Marblehead or the hilly Bald Knobs, carrying a rifle and looking for signs of deer. He searched among the spruce and birch for limbs rubbed raw by antlers, or flattened places in the grass where the herds would bed down.

It was on one such jaunt, during a foggy twilight, when Bubba drove his jeep along a narrow two-track and spotted a doe with twin yearling bucks. Bubba's rifle lay in the back seat of the jeep. With amazing dexterity for a man of his size, Bubba eased out of the jeep, and without alarming the deer, unzipped the rifle from its case, took aim, and fired. One of the bucks instantly collapsed into the tall grass.

Bubba put his rifle back in the case, took his hunting knife and walked through the mist to where the fallen deer lay. To his astonishment, the young buck was back on its feet, standing quietly as if waiting for him.

"Damn!" Bubba thought. "I could have sworn that was a clean shot!"

The rifle lay encased in the jeep. But there was a chance that the deer could still walk, so Bubba decided that the most humane thing would be to grab the young buck and dispatch it with his knife.

He dove on the deer, wrapping his arms around its neck and clutching his knife. The deer flipped on its side and pummeled Bubba with its hoofs. Bubba grunted, rolling on the ground with the flailing animal in an attempt to subdue it. But he didn't anticipate the strength of the deer. Its rock-hard, sharp hoofs kept whacking and thumping Bubba all up and down his ribs and on the side of his head.

"I've been in bar fights that were not as bad," Bubba said later. The deer struggled mightily, giving its assailant a few extra kicks for good measure, then broke free and trotted off into the brush.

Bubba lay on the cold ground for a moment. His sides ached and pain ripped through his head. He finally staggered to his feet, took a few steps back toward the jeep, and found the dead deer he had shot earlier.

He whirled around, but the young and healthy brother that he had just wrestled was long gone.

As I stood there remembering the story of Bubba's twin bucks, Bob's white-footed doe continued to regard me without fear. The whitetail population on Drummond had been thinned dramatically over the years, but certain individuals were amazingly tough. I decided to leave the doe alone. I put the horse treats on the ground for her and went back to my truck.

I wondered if I would dream that night.

Chapter Ten

"He who has a why to live can bear almost any how."
~Friedrich Nietzsche

One night while I was getting ready for bed, I could hear a familiar "huck, huck, huck" from downstairs. I heard Bruce call, "Reva's throwing up! I put her out."

A dog throwing up was not that unusual, but I came downstairs and went out the front door. I looked around and then spotted Reva sitting over by the truck. I thought it odd that she would be sitting there. "Come here," I said.

She got up and came over, but she was hunched as she moved. She was drooling profusely. I reached down and felt her abdomen; which was distended and really tight. As I stood there, she began attempting to vomit again, with her head down, sides heaving, but with no results.

Bruce came out of the house. I turned to him. "Will you stay out here with her? I have to call a vet. I think this is bloat."

I called two emergency clinics and finally found one open in Ann Arbor. They said bring her right away. Reva was very uncomfortable, shifting around, and I could see the pain in her eyes. Her belly seemed to be getting bigger by the minute, and was gurgling and rumbling. I had never seen a case of bloat, or torsion as they called it., but I'd heard that the dog's stomach turns upside down. I picked Reva up and put her into the back of the Sonoma, dubbed the RevaBus, and ran to the front and jumped in. Bruce drove, ambling slowly down the driveway.

I said, "I drive faster than this going to the movies! You have to HURRY!"

"I don't want to toss Reva around."

"Toss her around! At least she'll be alive!"

It took nearly an hour to get to the clinic. When we arrived, Reva was sitting near the back of the truck, leaning against the tailgate. She hopped out, and she looked pregnant. Both sides were bulging noticeably by now, and she was sick. Her eyes glazed in pain and she moved slowly. We took her in, they did an X-ray, and sure enough the stomach had inverted and she needed immediate surgery.

"Your dog has torsion," Dr. Ben said. "Of course we can go in and see how it looks, but in a dog her age, especially one that's had problems as she had, it might not be good. If I go in and her organs look bad, it might be best not to awaken her."

I realized that this was a formality, and he had to prepare us for the worst. But meanwhile, I was thinking, "Yeah, right, whatever, just get her UNDER, already, she HURTS!"

Fortunately he had the perception to see me shifting uncomfortably, and read what I was thinking. He said, "Well, I'll scrub up and do my best for her."

"Thank you! Can I watch the surgery?" I said.

He smiled a little. "No, that's not a good idea. You'll make me nervous, and I need to concentrate. You just sit tight. We'll take good care of her."

The next two hours seemed excruciating, but I was thinking that it was a good thing he hadn't come out right away and announced that her organs looked bad.

Finally, the door opened and he came out, still in scrubs and with the mask hanging at his throat like a bib. "Her internal organs looked very healthy for a thirteen year old dog, and her prognosis is good. I tacked her stomach to the wall of her abdominal cavity, which may help prevent it from happening again."

I had been optimistic, but could not restrain a sigh of relief. "Why does it happen?"

"We don't know exactly why bloat occurs, but the stomach is always full when it happens. They used to think it was caused by dogs eating too fast, and/or exercising after a meal, but this wasn't the case with Reva. For awhile there was a theory that the spleen interfered with the stomach somehow, causing it to flip, but since Reva no longer HAS a spleen...."

"Yes, it was taken out, along with a tumor, last fall."

He grinned. "Boy, when we picked her up to move her, I couldn't believe the way her hips were popping and creaking!"

I laughed and said, "I know. But she just keeps going, and going, and going...."

"Well, attitude has a lot to do with recovery. She may be one of those dogs who says, 'Why did you SEW me shut? Why didn't you just VELCRO me back together? It would be easier to get me open for the next one!'"

We left her in his care, and went home then. It was four in the morning, but I didn't go back to bed. I was too wound up. Later that day, I called to check on her, but she had spiked a fever, and they wouldn't release her. "You can come and visit her though," the receptionist said.

"No, she'll see me and expect to come home. I can't do that to her."

I waited. They gave her antibiotics, and a shot to bring the fever down, and the next day I went to pick her up. I stood in the waiting room by the counter, wondering how she was going to be feeling. Then, the door to the back room popped open, and a grizzled black snout shoved out. That was all I could see, just a demanding snout, sniffing the air. A moment later it disappeared.

I smiled. It was all I needed to know. Sure enough, a minute later, the door burst open and out plunged Reva, panting hard and dragging a veterinary technician behind her. She greeted me briefly, and then, as I grabbed the leash, she pulled me quickly toward the exit.

Chapter Eleven

"What you are thunders so that I cannot hear what you say to the contrary."
~ Ralph Waldo Emerson

"Is your husband seeing another woman?"

Coming from a plastic surgeon, this question left me a little taken aback. I did not answer him right away, and he correctly took my silence as affirmation.

"And is she younger?"

It was eerie, the things he could read. She was also taller, wore lots of makeup, and had a conventional office job. The thought of her made me queasy. Worst of all, she had been a friend of mine, and had come over recently for a birthday party. We had sat together in a group, laughing, while Bruce took pictures of us. It was, of course, before I'd found out. I could feel my face growing warm. I looked down. "She had cake with me."

It couldn't have made sense to him, but he seemed to be reading the entire story in my face. "I see."

"What does that have to do with fixing my nose?"

"Your nose doesn't need fixing. There's nothing wrong with it."

"The nostrils don't match." I pointed to them helpfully.

"That's hardly noticeable. When was your accident?"

"One year ago."

"You have healed beautifully. You don't need a nose job."

"But what about this?" I pointed to the long scar running between my nose and mouth.

"You can't really see it. Actually you're not that good a candidate for surgery, because of all the damage to your cartilage. Your nose was crushed on one side, like an eggshell. Reconstruction might cause it to collapse again."

It was my fourth visit to him. Each time I had pleaded and begged for rhinoplasty, only to be rebuffed. I couldn't believe he was refusing me. After all, insurance was supposed to cover it, and didn't he want to be paid? Wasn't this his job?

That night on the phone, Kimmy asked how it had gone.

"He says I don't need a plastic surgeon, I need a shrink!"

"That is totally unprofessional!" she roared. "Get a second opinion."

"I like him. I actually like the fact that he is hesitant to do it. He has good morals."

"He's nosy and manipulative if you ask me!" she snorted.

"No pun intended, eh?"

"You don't need a nose job! I have to admit that he's right. Don't think you can save your marriage by changing your appearance."

"I don't think that. I just want a nose job."

"Is Bruce still seeing her?"

"According to him, no."

She then launched into a tirade of epithets about liars and cheaters, while I sat back and winced. Finally, she paused, and I changed the subject. "I didn't get that job."

"What?"

"Yeah, remember I interviewed with this company my friend Melissa works for? She's a graphic artist."

I knew how to interview. I had put on a suit, gone in and sat at a long table below the quietly humming, jittery fluorescent lights. I laughed at all their jokes, made eye contact and used a firm handshake. I had the stellar record of having acquired every job I'd ever interviewed for.

The whole time, I found myself wishing I was hiding in the woods. I had been out of the work force for ten years. It was nauseating. I didn't want to be there, but I'd sold myself with my best professional fervor. They deliberated for three weeks, then told me I was overqualified. Melissa was crushed. I was elated.

"Are you nuts?" Kimmy said. "Don't get a job. That won't save your marriage. Look at me. I worked for sixteen years and what good did it do me?"

"I just thought it would be a good idea to do it now before things fall apart."

"Don't waste your time in some piddly office! Girl, if I had even one iota of your talent, I'd be filthy rich by now!"

I had heard Kimmy say that so many times, I could lip sync it.

"Do watercolors," she commanded. "That's what sells."

"I can't work with watercolors. They're too hard."

"Don't give me that!" she barked. "I still have that painting of the horse you did back in college. Remember, the one I pulled out of the trash?"

"I can't believe you still have that thing!"

That was how I'd met Kimmy. She was a Criminal Justice student who had been assigned to janitorial duty on her work study program. She cleaned the women's dorms every day. She had found the rejected, slightly rumpled watercolor in the wastebasket sitting outside my room one early morning. She confronted me later, holding up the painting and telling me I "should have more respect for a God-given talent."

She had been pulling my morale out of the trash ever since.

"I had it framed," she said.

"I know." I shook my head and laughed. "I think that was the last time I used watercolors. That was twenty years ago."

She was right about watercolors selling, though. In the days when I used to do art shows, people always asked for them. I could understand why. I loved the way watercolor looked when used by those more skillful than I; the way the thin layers of color blended and formed to create images with depth and light and shadow, a medium so unique and unmistakable.

But I didn't like working with watercolors. For me, the paint dripped uncontrollably on the paper and spread at random. There was no stopping a wave of watercolor once it started. And once I made them, my mistakes remained. Layering over them could sometimes make them less visible, but upon close inspection, there they were. They were just like the scars on my face.

I stuck with pastels and acrylics, things that could be corrected; covered with another layer. They were safer.

"I am giving up on art. I need to get a job like a normal person."

"Bailey, don't you dare give up your art. People who ignore their talent are spitting in God's face."

"If I get a job, there won't be any time for art."

"There must be some way to keep your talent from going to waste. Lots of people would pay good money for what you can do."

"Point them out!"

"Don't you get smart with me!" she laughed.

"Talent is nice, but it won't save my marriage," I said.

"You can't win Bruce back by trying to become the other woman. He needs to love you for who you are."

"I'm not doing that!"

"Yes you are."

"No I'm not."

"Are too."

"Am not."

"Yes you are. It's just the same as when you tried to cook the beans that time, remember? Don't bother! He doesn't appreciate you!"

"Kimmy, are you still drinking?"

"Of course I am, you dodo, it's for my back pain. But I don't get drunk anymore. I have a tolerance."

"You need to quit that."

"Stop changing the subject. Look, just forget them both. Let her have Bruce if she wants him! They can toodle off into the sunset in the Land of Mediocrity."

"I don't want a divorce! And I don't want to have to sell my horses."

"Why would you have to?"

"I couldn't support them on my own. I could barely support myself."

"You always land on your feet. Just trust your gut, and you'll be fine."

"I hope you're right."

"You know I am. Let's just put up a house on my land up in Manistique. We'll have horses and dogs and you can draw and write and I'll make jewelry."

"We have to wait until Makayla grows up. We'll be old by then."

"That's even better. I'll get a shotgun and we can sit in our rockers. I want to be an old eccentric bag lady."

"Well, you're partway there."

She laughed uproariously. "You always make me feel better! Don't change your nose, Bailey. Don't change a thing."

"I have to change. I have to be tougher. I know it's in me."

Chapter Twelve

"'Tis very certain the desire of life prolongs it."
~ Lord Byron

My mom's mother was a hundred years old. She was a thin, soft-spoken lady who liked to wear dresses in alarming neon colors, and pumps to match. She had emigrated from Sweden with her parents when she was a child, married at eighteen, and lost her husband when she was twenty-nine. She never remarried. She had raised eight kids on her own, washing and hanging people's clothes to make a living. She moved to Arizona later in life, but came back to northern Michigan and stayed with my folks every summer.

One August night, she was sleeping in the master bedroom. It was past midnight and I sat in the kitchen writing a letter, enjoying the quiet, while Reva slept at my feet. The only sound was the ticking of the ancient wooden clock which hung crookedly on the wall above me.

Reva was just a year old at that time. Despite her state of clumsy adolescence, she could emit a deep, ferocious bark. At that moment she did, waking from a sound sleep, thundering loud enough to shake the windows. I nearly dropped my pen. She leaped up and charged across the room, just as I heard my Grandmother's voice saying, "No! Get out!"

Reva forced the bedroom door open, and to my horror, burst inside, barking like mad. I ran in after her, and the hallway's beam of light revealed Grandma sitting straight up in bed. Reva stood next to the bed with her nose up on the pillow, nudging and licking Grandma's hands.

"Grandma! I am so sorry! I've no idea what's come over her!"

"Did you see that?" Grandma pointed toward me with a gnarled, trembly finger.

"What?"

"There was someone here!"

I smiled. "Oh no Grandma, no one is here. I am still up, there's nobody in this house. You were having a dream."

"No, there was."

"Can I get you anything?"

She sighed, her shoulders sagging a little in resignation. "No thank you."

"Okay, good night then. Everything's okay. Come on, Reva."

Reva came out of the room and I softly closed the door.

The next morning, Dad took me aside and said, "What happened with your grandmother last night?"

"Reva went bursting into her room and woke her up. Grandma was upset, too. She was having a bad dream that she saw someone."

Dad turned and looked at me over the top of his glasses. "She did see someone. She said it was a man, with a long white beard, in a white robe, standing at the foot of her bed."

I felt the foggy chill that comes only with the supernatural. "What? Who was it?"

"She doesn't know. She was telling him to go away. He disappeared when your dog came in."

We never found out who the apparition was, or why he was there. I felt badly that I hadn't listened to Grandma more closely that night. She never again spoke of her strange visitor, .but she continued to thwart the Grim Reaper for the next four years. And from that time on, she would sneak Reva tidbits under the table.

Chapter Thirteen

"Any man that doesn't love a horse, there is something the matter with that man!"
~ *Will Rogers*

I bought a new used bridle and breast collar for Dad to use in the 4th of July parade. I was so excited because the set was loaded with silver and has a long romel rein. The leather was soft and dark and pliable. I have never owned anything so nice.

I got the bit installed one night and tried the set on Clifford. Even without a bath, and in the evening half-light, he glowed with all that silver.

Since I had him tacked up, the dogs would have been mighty disappointed if I didn't take him for a little ride. So I climbed aboard the duded-up Clifford, and the Canine Caravan followed us down the long and winding driveway. We were serenaded by tree frogs and other chirping things. It was cool and gradually growing dark but that silver still gleamed.

I had owned Clifford for six years by this time, and had kept a journal of his antics. Every time he did something new and funny, I would send it to the Morgan horse discussion list on the Internet. People started eagerly awaiting the next Clifford story, and finally someone asked, "When is the book coming out?"

I'd had a flashback to my childhood. I was sitting at my desk, writing on lined notebook paper, writing hundreds of pages of horse stories and drawing pictures to go with them.

Of course! A Clifford book. It seemed like a self-fulfilling prophecy. It just felt like the right thing to do.

I had started compiling the stories that fall, forsaking my job hunt to sit for hours at the computer and type.

"You're wasting your time!" Bruce had said.

"I'm sure you're right." But I'd kept on writing.

Clifford, the dogs and I got back to the barn, and I dismounted and carefully removed the new treasures. As I squatted down to tuck them back into the new quilted bridle bag, I felt something warm on the back of my neck. I paused, realizing it was Clifford's nose. I sat still, and it remained, quiet and warm, not blowing in my hair, just buried there and resting softly. I waited. Finally, after a long minute, I began to giggle and the nose moved up to my ear and cheek and blew a light breath. I turned, kissed him on the white diamond there, and he flipped his lip to kiss me back.

Chapter Fourteen

*"Strength does not come from a physical capacity.
It comes from an indomitable will."*
~ Mahatma Gandhi

Reva was throwing up again. Worried that it might be another case of bloat, I took her in to see Cheryl. It was late December.

"Was she just trying to get one more surgery in before the end of the year, or what?" Cheryl said, palpating Reva's abdomen.

She looked in Reva's mouth. "Here's the problem. She's cracked a tooth."

"How in the heck did she do that?"

"Probably chewing on a stick or something."

"I can't think of when she's had a stick recently. She hasn't been out much."

"Well, with dogs, ya just never know. Anyway, you'll have to leave her here. I'll put her under and take that thing out."

The surgery went without a problem, and Reva came home that night.

"What is it with your family and tooth problems?" Kimmy said. "At least they fixed yours."

"Yeah, after two root canals and four crowns. You shoulda seen em when they ground em down. Picket fence. Yuck."

"You'd have looked like someone on a talk show."

I started laughing.

"I'm not kidding!" she said. "If a tooth pops out, you automatically lose ninety percent of your brain."

I had ground up canned food for Reva and put water in it. She was eating it as we chatted. Her mouth was so sore she couldn't really chew, so she was lapping up the gruel.

Cajun, the young German shepherd who now outweighed Reva by about ten pounds, was trying to get me to play ball with him. He was picking it up and throwing it down, letting it bounce. Then he chased it and picked it up and threw it again. It rolled over next to the dish Reva was eating from. It bounced off the dish and then rested there. Reva kept eating. Cajun was faced with the obvious quandary. He looked at the ball, then up at me, then at the ball again.

I laughed. "NOW what are you going to do?"

He gave up and walked away.

Chapter Fifteen

"When hospitality becomes an art, it loses its very soul."
~ Max Beerbohm

"I have people coming to look at Zach, for their eleven year old daughter. It's a wonderful home! They keep horses forever! But they will want Clifford, not Zach." I set the phone back in its cradle and looked at Bruce.

"Clifford's not for sale," he said, with a confused expression.

"Right. But they're going to decide to go with a horse like him. Clifford is nine years old, little and bomb proof. He's what you think of as the kid's horse. They won't take Zach. They'll keep looking. Clifford's going to kill the sale."

"Just don't get him out while they are here."

"Well. I guess I don't need to. Clifford will be awfully disappointed though."

Susan showed up with her husband Tom and a lovely daughter, Samantha. We chatted about horses as we made our way through the snow to the barn. I had left Reva in the house because the ground was slippery and wet, and her eyesight was weakening. I worried that with guests around, I might not be able to keep a close eye on her. But Cajun and Scorch, and Gus the rescued Corgi mix, were glad to have the company.

Zach came out of the stall a true gentleman, and was his usual quiet self. I tacked him up and Susan remarked on how he looked like a gelding she'd owned. I led him outside and got on. Despite the wet, slushy snow, he walked around the yard calmly and did some nice leg yields.

"He's so cute!" Susan said.

After Zach had gone through his paces awhile, I said, "Want to try him out?"

"Sure!" Samantha climbed on while I held Zach. She clucked to him and he ambled off, only to return to stand in front of me.

"He sort of has a problem with low self-esteem," I said. "He really just needs someone to love him and spend time with him."

"Samantha's an intermediate rider," Susan explained. "She's taking lessons, and the horse we buy is going to go right into training for the 4H shows."

How wonderful this would be! The little girl was so gentle and seemed to have a truly kind nature. After she had ridden him for awhile, she dismounted and led him back in the barn. Out of the corner of my eye, I saw Clifford stirring impatiently in his stall as we walked by.

Zach stood in the aisle with his head pressed against Samantha's chest. She whispered to him and stroked his face while I took the saddle off. I did a double take, glancing over at him. His posture was stooped, his ears out sadly to the sides. I felt like I could read his mind. He seemed to be pleading with the little girl. "Please, save me from this terrible place!"

"Ungrateful..." I muttered.

Susan laughed. "There's just no loyalty, is there?"

I grinned. They really were nice folks. And if Zach wanted to play the pathetic routine, fine. They could feel sorry for him, and take him home.

Clifford rattled his feed bucket. The dogs panted happily around our knees.

Susan walked over to look in at Trudy who stood quietly watching the proceedings. "She's really pretty."

I led Zach back into his stall and removed the halter. "Thank you. Everyone always loves Trudy. And she deserves it. She is a very good girl."

I slid Zach's door shut as Susan went over to look at Clifford. "So, this is Clifford."

"Yes," I said, glancing in at him. He snapped his lips, nodding his head wickedly, pawing the stall floor.

"We've read all the stories about him on the internet! When is the book going to be published?"

"It should be out later in the spring." I put the saddle away and then stepped over next to her. His ears popped forward when I walked up. "Oh, he is asking to come out." I sighed.

I just couldn't disappoint him. He had already waited over an hour, even sort of patiently. Besides, we didn't have much company in the winter. "Would you like to see his tricks?"

"Yes! That would be great!" The family gathered around me eagerly. I opened Clifford's stall door and let him out. He pinned his ears and quickly surveyed each visitor rudely.

"He won't bite," I tried to explain. "Sometimes he makes ugly faces. My dad taught him...."

But Susan had grabbed her child and pulled her back a step.

Clifford leered unpleasantly, snorting, and then turned his back on the guests and wandered down the aisle. "Come here," I said.

He came back and I tossed his orange cone out the door. He went peeling after it, to the great joy of the dogs, who raced around in the snow barking at him. Clifford crossly picked up the cone and started back with it. It was wet and slipped out of his teeth. He reached down to pick it up again as Gus the Corgi mix leaped and yammered around his face.

Clifford straightened up, ears pinned, eyes rolling, and thrust the cone skyward, shaking his head at the lunging, braying dog in front of him. At that moment I wished I had let Reva out after all, as she would certainly have run interference. Gus didn't move, and continued to bark, so Clifford picked up one front foot and rapped him sharply on the top of the skull. Gus stood for a moment, apparently dazed, staring into space, as Clifford trotted irritably past him. After a brief moment of what seemed like deep contemplation, Gus shook his head and came charging happily into the barn.

As Clifford delivered the cone to my hand, Tom said, "Did you see that? He just stomped that dog."

Susan forced a smile. "That was a really nice trick. Very cute."

She clutched her daughter a little more closely against her as Clifford waited impatiently for the next toss.

"He stomped that dog," Tom insisted. He turned to look after Gus, who was at the end of the barn aisle now, digging through the hay bales in search of mice.

Susan cast a pitying look over toward Zach's stall, but seemed to catch herself. She kept smiling determinedly. "Well, we really should be getting home now. Thank you so much for your time, and for the nice visit."

"Oh, sure, any time." I opened up the stall door and Clifford trotted grumpily back in. "Thanks for coming."

"We'll let you know what we decide about Zach," Susan clutched her child's hand and walked swiftly up the hill to the driveway. Tom picked up his video camera and stole another glance at Gus before fleeing after her.

I waved as they pulled away, and gave them my most hospitable smile.

They never came back.

Chapter Sixteen

"Education consists mainly of what we have unlearned."
~ Mark Twain

I was delighted when clicker training was brought to an Equine Expo in Lansing that year. Vincent and Shauna Karrasch gave a brilliant demo that accurately showed how the clicker works with horses. I thought it was high time the method became recognized for its potential with equines.

The clicker method was invented by dolphin trainers, who used a whistle as an "event marker" to tell the animal that food was coming. They would blow a whistle at the height of a dolphin's jump, so that the dolphin understood at that moment what was going to be rewarded. It was all in the timing, and there was no coercion involved. The click worked the same way.

A clicker was a small plastic "cricket" or child's toy, adapted for dog training. If I wanted to teach a dog to sit, I clicked when his rump hit the floor. If I wanted to teach him to come when called, I clicked when he moved toward me. The dog understood that the treat would soon follow. But it was the timing of the click that was the crucial thing.

With this clear and simple form of communication, one could teach an animal to do virtually anything it was physically capable of doing.

When I'd acquired Clifford as an unruly two-year-old, I had already been teaching dogs with the clicker for a number of years so it seemed a natural adaptation to work with him. He was now a veteran clicker student, and learned things more quickly than some of the dogs I'd worked with.

I was excited to be going to see a public demo with horses. But I laughed when Shauna, a former whale trainer at a seaquarium, used huge gestures to signal her horse, waving her arms like a cheerleader to get him to back across the arena or walk on three legs. I knew a horse, being a prey animal, had very good eyesight and could see and respond to a wriggled finger as a cue.

The big gestures seemed grandiose to me – until I realized that, when the function is to demonstrate before a crowd, these types of signals were probably necessary in order for the audience to see and understand the training concepts.

The demonstration was inspiring to me.

To my delight, they had fashioned a target stick for horses, out of a round wooden handle with a white bobber on the end – the floatation device used to hold fish nets.

Targeting was a great tool for any animal. If a horse learned to target effectively, he could be moved this way or that, taught to come when called, taught to stand still for shoeing or grooming. The uses of a target were many and varied. Best of all, targeting was perhaps the quickest way to teach any animal the concept of the click and treat method.

I quickly bought one of those sticks.

I spent that Saturday evening in the barn, teaching my horses to touch the new target stick. The first session, of course, was with Clifford who had to be creative. He tried biting it, taking it away from me, butting it with his head, and pawing it with his foot. Apparently he thought a mere touch wasn't good enough. We quickly graduated to me trying to re-teach the bow with it; asking him to hold one foot in the air while simultaneously touching the target on the ground with his nose. He got the idea, but never did bow all the way down.

I moved on to Zach, who eyed the target suspiciously at first, then, slowly and ever so gently moved his nostrils to blow on it. He would get a fraction of an inch from it, and blow. I clicked him for that,
because it was close, then he figured I just wanted him to blow on the target. I guess he knew he had a birthday coming up.

Trudy touched it immediately, and then when I clicked and treated her, she figured it was trick time, so she resorted to her one trick -- smiling. She grinned and touched, grinned and touched, her big yellow teeth beaming around that target like an Osmond at the microphone.

Cajun shoved each stall door open, watching jealously. He had seen that target stick and knew right away what it was, although it was about ten times the size of his doggy target stick. When I came out of the stall with it, he jumped on me and bumped it so hard he nearly knocked me over. Since he wanted it so badly, I let him touch it a few times, but he didn't want praise or petting, only to touch the stick again. Unfortunately, to the horses, the behavior wasn't that self-reinforcing. They wanted to be paid. Maybe they were just smarter.

Clifford was a terrible mugger. Throughout his life, his "event marker" was inadvertently the crackling cellophane of the peppermints which my dad fed him every summer. Dad was unknowingly reinforcing head swinging, leering, ear pinning, lip thumping behavior which became more and more extreme as time went on.

Since Clifford had probably killed Zach's sale to a good home, I realized that these ugly faces had to stop. He scared people. Not only that, but the faces themselves seemed to promote an impatient attitude. One day, when I was working on teaching him to back on cue from the ground, he snaked his neck out and made as if to nip me on the arm. It wasn't an actual bite, being more of a punch with his nose. But it was quick and he'd made his point. I wasn't delivering the treats fast enough for him.

I promptly turned around and left the corral, and he had to stay there alone for the rest of the afternoon. I called this, "Packing up my Barbies and going home."

I started working on free leading, teaching him to "heel" by my side much as a dog does. I might go one step forward, one back, one left, one right. The movement kept him from getting too bored. Meanwhile, I kept my hand in the fanny pack and rustled around in there constantly, saturating him with the noise of crackling plastic. He was never reinforced during the times when he had his nose toward me. I clicked only during times he was looking away. He never made as if to bite me again, but if he stomped or did anything too extreme, I packed up my Barbies.

It didn't take long at all for him to learn to swing his head away from me. After that, I began asking for forward ears.

The transformation was amazing! In a few weeks, he became quiet and tolerant, standing patiently while I walked all around him, free leading nicely at my side with no more bumping, head swinging, or ugly faces. It was really incredible how reinforcing the "Not-Mugging" also seemed to help his attitude.

He still, however, made ugly faces at Dad.

Chapter Seventeen

"Ambition is the germ from which all growth of nobleness proceeds."
~ Thomas Dunn English

I decided to start tracking with Cajun again early that spring. He was now a two year old shepherd, still in the throes of adolescence, but becoming a giant. He was beautifully colored, with rich black and red pigment, dark eyes that snapped with fun, and a square, blocky head that was all male. He exuded joyous energy, almost too much to be just a pet.

His brother, Cavar, who had grown up with us, was now a police dog in the Detroit K9 unit. While still a rookie, Cavar had been the first dog to win the Medal of Valor when he tracked down a mass murderer who was hiding on the roof of a garage.

Cajun was made of the same stuff – always busy, always thinking. Keeping him occupied was part of my job in living with him. I taught him tricks, and played Frisbee, and we took agility classes. Now we were tracking again.

I didn't know if he would remember what to do, since it had been fall when I quit tracking with him -- probably early October sometime. But when he saw me take that leather glove out of the closet, that was all he needed. He let out an excited squeal and tried to grab it.

I left him in the house and walked out into the pasture. I trampled around on a patch of ground about three feet in diameter, creating a scent pad which signified the start of the trail. Then I walked a straight line about fifty yards, turned sharp left and walked another fifty. Finally after making another turn, I left the glove hidden in a stubbly patch of weeds between three old manure piles. Then I came back, being careful not to walk over the trail I had just laid.

He was waiting eagerly by the door when I came back in. I quietly put his harness on while he stood and wailed and quivered with anticipation. I clipped the long line to his harness, and he put his nose to the ground as soon as we crossed the threshold.

I could tell he was a little rusty, as we hit the pasture he progressed more slowly than usual -- but that was a good thing. I had been trying to explain to him that the object was NOT to gallop along at top speed with his nose to the ground.

It was windy, and there was a lot of old manure, so my scent was blowing around and mixing with strong old manure smell. But he tracked me in the huge U-shape all the way across the field. His head was down, tail up and waving industriously as he sniffed deeply in the grass. I followed at the end of the line, about ten feet behind him, wondering again at the mysterious power of the canine olfactory sense.

He almost missed the first corner, and I had to let the line go tight while I stopped and waited for him to pick the scent up. But he found it and we were off.

He made the second turn with no problem. I had camouflaged the glove too well in the midst of that manure scent. It was difficult for him, and he bypassed it. I had to stop and wait, while he made circles and contaminated the track. But finally, after walking practically on top of it, he did find the glove and picked it up. I unhooked him and he went galloping triumphantly off with it, shaking it and play-bowing at me, teasing me with it. I chased him a little; he loved that.

I went looking for his tennis ball which had been in the garage. I figured I would trade that for the glove so he wouldn't destroy it.

I couldn't find the ball. Disgusted with myself for being unprepared, I found some dog biscuits to use as trade. When I turned around, he had both glove and tennis ball in his mouth, and was looking at me expectantly.

Chapter Eighteen

"Those who believe a dog has no soul have never looked into the eyes of a German shepherd."
~ *Unknown*

That spring, I opened the door to see a flat brown box on the front porch. "Amazon.com" was marked in black letters across it. I tore it open, and pulled out a book, a trade paperback with a glossy black cover. The photo of Clifford and Reva walking together on the sand was splashed across the cover, along with the big white letters spelling, "Clifford of Drummond Island". My heart raced. I sat down and flipped through it, looked at the pages, all bits of familiar stories, family names, places mentioned and the illustrations I had redone.

I had to catch my breath. I felt as though my entire life was peaking at this moment – it had all led to this. It was a completely wonderful feeling.

Not long afterward, Bruce filed for divorce. He moved out of the house, and I began to hear stories from friends about his public appearances with the Other Woman. I couldn't take it. I had to get away. I loaded up Clifford and Trudy and headed north. I wanted to spend the summer on Drummond Island, taking refuge under the pretense of promoting my book.

During those first few days, I felt completely at peace. I had some direction in life with my writing, and realized I was finally free of the cloud of criticism. I took walks with the dogs out to Reva's Lake, but on the way back,

Reva kept stopping to rest. We took our time, but I could tell that despite her active lifestyle, something was wrong and she wasn't up to going that distance anymore.

I took her for little walks around camp, and still saddled up Clifford and went for short rides so that she could trot along. She stayed right next to his right hind leg, as always, with her big old-dog grin.

Then on the fifth of July, when I pulled in to camp and opened the tailgate, and the dogs jumped out, Reva jumped out too and she collapsed. She lay on her side, not moving. I rushed to her, and she blinked and looked around.

She sat up, then immediately stiffened and fell over again. I felt her heart, and she didn't seem to be breathing. I sat with her, petting her, and then she gave a huge gasp, and raised her head.

"It's okay," I said. "You can go if you need to. We'll be okay. You've done well. You're a good girl."

I kept my voice level and calm. She hated it when I got upset.

She sat up, panting hard, and looked around. I watched her for a minute, and she collapsed again. She always fell in the same direction, toward the left. Her head tilted backward and she became very stiff. She struggled to breathe.

This seizure was a long, hard one, and when she woke up she was very weak. By that time I had gotten on the cell phone. There was no veterinary office on the island, but there was a retired one who sometimes came out in emergencies.

While I waited for him to arrive, Reva came to and stood up shakily. She looked around. I gave her some water and she drank it, and shook herself.

"Okay then," I said. "You want to stay?"

I went to the corral and got Clifford. I led him over to the horse trailer and put the saddle on him. Reva shadowed him as always, and sat and watched with her old intensity. I smiled.

The vet pulled up. "What's the matter, here? You have an old dog that needs to be put to sleep?"

"I don't think so, after all," I said.

He got out of the truck and Reva went up to him and barked. Watching her move, he said, "Oh, her hips are a mess! She's in pain."

"I know, but we control it with her medication. She's been motoring along like this for awhile now."

He shook his head, looking at her. "She really should be put to sleep."

"She's not ready," I said, giving Clifford a pat. Reva was sitting there, looking at me, and suddenly her head thrust backward and she collapsed.

"Oh, no." I said.

The seizure was long and hard, and she lay stiff and still and not breathing.

"Okay," I said to the vet. He had the injection ready, and my old friend died in my arms, just a few feet from where Clifford was standing.

I covered her with some saddle blankets; Clifford's special purple one that we had used for many years, which sometimes served as her bed in the back of the truck. Clifford stood waiting, and I got on and we rode down to the bay, to hear the gulls and watch the sun go down behind the trees. As I rode, I didn't look down toward his right hind leg. I could feel her there. I knew that her spirit lived on, that she was in touch with that world. After all, while she was alive, she had gone after ghosts.

Chapter Nineteen

*"For where your treasure is,
there will your heart be also."*
~ Matthew 6:21

There was no way to describe the cavern that Reva's absence created. She was a definite presence that defined a sort of consistency in our days. She watched over all of us. Clifford did not seem to acknowledge that she was gone, and continued to munch hay with aplomb. I went into the corral one afternoon and looked at him, and he at me, and I said, "I need you."

He seemed to know. He came over and put his head in the halter, and allowed me to lead him out and saddle him up. We rode out by Huron Bay that day, Scorch and Cajun racing ahead and crashing through the woods after squirrels as always. The northwoods were majestic as ever, but to look down by Clifford's right hind leg revealed no German shepherd there in her usual place. It was awful.

We came to a stop by the dead cedar where I always tied Clifford, near the steps of rocks that lead down to the shoreline. I got off and went down by the shore to find some sticks while Cajun and Scorch romped beside me. The waves crashed against the rocks, again and again with their own loose rhythm, lulling me into a sense of familiar comfort. As I threw sticks in for the dogs, I heard a squeal. I looked up, and there stood Clifford, tied to his tree as always.

His head was up, eyes searching the surrounding shoreline. His nostrils flared. He called again.

It was at that moment I realized what was wrong. Reva had always stayed with Clifford while the other dogs swam. But today he was alone. He had been left behind, and today there was no Reva to sit beside him, watching his every move intently, making sure he did not leave his position, making
sure that he was safe. Clifford stomped his foot impatiently, swished his tail and shifted his hindquarters around so he could look behind him toward the woods. Another deep, rumbling whinny poured from him, his ribs quivering with the effort of his call.

I started to walk toward him, but his eyes roamed beyond me, searching with growing panic. He screamed and screamed, his calls echoing with heartbreaking resonance over the tossing green water of Huron Bay, sounding off into the distance, heralding an answering bark from the one who could answer no more.

I recognized then that his signs of grief, of missing her, were more subtle than my own. The dogs had buried their noses into her grave, sniffing deeply, and seemed satisfied. Clifford had stood close by and watched her die. But there was a subdued air about him for the days that followed. He had lost that familiar roguish spark. He did not tease. He did not give me any trouble at all. He behaved with perfect manners, a gentleman, kind and cooperative.

Trudy was less affected, having little use for dogs of any sort. She tolerated them, that was all. They seemed to cramp her style. She took great pride in being a lady at all times, and dogs just didn't fit into that role.

That evening when we rode down to Clifford's Bay, I let her run along. She trotted, high-stepping and prim, along with us. We came out of the woods and walked along the sand, splashing gently through the water to the gravel shoal. I sat aboard Clifford and looked out across the bay, remembering the many happy times we had spent there.

Trudy gave a little snort, and I looked over to see her toying with a bright yellow piece of rope, apparently a scrap from someone's boat. She was rubbing it back and forth on the ground with her nose. I turned Clifford and we splashed back to the beach. It was quiet, late afternoon, with the sun sending long shadows across the sand, and the softest breeze blowing. Cajun and Scorch panted and splashed happily. Clifford walked quietly, head down. I looked back. There stood Trudy, on the shoal, watching us with her dark head high and that bright yellow rope dangling from her mouth.

I stopped. She swung her head, twirling that rope, and then gave a squeal. Up flung her heels and she leapt into the water. The rope went flying. Clifford's head popped up and he watched as she came barreling toward us, knocking water high all around her. He nickered an answer and bounded
forward with no bidding from me. And then we were running after her, with Trudy bucking and snorting on the shoreline, bright water flying about like confetti, her dark coat gleaming in the sun like bittersweet chocolate, mane and tail flying.

We ran and the dogs ran with us, barking, with the wind whipping past us, surrounded by sand and blue water and golden evening light. I would never forget those moments -- some of the most beautiful in my life.

From that day, Clifford resumed his stealing and teasing habits, and Trudy reverted back to her ladylike self. I marveled at this mare, her amazing ability to pull this role reversal and play the clown when we needed it most.

Chapter Twenty

"Intuition is a spiritual faculty and does not explain, but simply points the way."
~ Florence Scovel Shinn

I didn't stay up North that year.

With the loss of Reva, reality was hitting me hard. I had three horses to feed, and once the divorce was final, I'd have no income other than the alimony that Bruce had allotted me. I was forty years old and had been out of the work force for over ten years. I didn't have a college degree. I was beginning to feel an edge of panic. My dream of being a published writer had come true, but I wasn't selling enough Clifford books to pay the bills.

I decided that part of my problem was I had just too many mouths to feed.

Gus the Corgi mix had gone to live with some good friends of mine. I had placed Patty's two Papillons in a home with an older couple. They had an eight year old, fat Golden retriever who was very gentle, and they promised that Buzz and L.B. would stay together always. They sent me frequent updates and photos of the two. I thought Patty would have liked them.

When I tearfully told Kimmy that I had finally placed the dogs, she roared, "Isn't that just like a man! He ditches you for a younger woman and forces you to split up the family! Just be grateful you didn't have human kids, Bailey. You were smart."

"I don't know how you do it," I said.

"How long can you stay in the house?"

"Five years."

"Then it has to be sold, or what?"

"Yeah."

"Hrm," I heard her exhale, and knew she was smoking.

"I thought you were going to quit smoking."

"I thought you were going to quit nagging." She laughed. "Listen Bailey, you'll be okay. You always land on your feet."

"I just hope I can get a home for Zach," I said.

Zach was expensive to keep, eating twice as much as Clifford and Trudy combined. Though he ate so much, over the winter he had gotten thin and always looked a little hungry.

I decided to double my efforts to find a buyer for him. The first step was to get him to a professional trainer, someone who could deal with his low self esteem issues without making him worse.

I took him to a Morgan trainer who lived not far from me, Sandy Crechiolo.

Sandy was diminutive and sweet-looking, with a round face and freckles and happy brown eyes. Her most endearing feature was her voice, which squeaked and resonated through hills and valleys when she spoke. However, despite the fact that she looked and sounded like a kid, she had a no-nonsense way of handling horses that I liked.

From the beginning, Sandy wrote me long emails about Zach's progress that made me think of something a parent might receive from an elementary schoolteacher:

July 4, 2001

Hi Nancy,

Zach is doing very well. As he learns more about the mechanics of his balance, he is becoming more relaxed. I have been cantering him for the last couple of days. Only a few strides the first time, then around the arena a couple of times the second day. Little pieces at a time to let him get confident.

Even though he is 6, he feels like a green 3 yr old under saddle. He really doesn't understand about his body position or balance. This is one of the biggest things that causes him to be stiff. He has been
100% in his work ethic and his desire to try. He has been learning at a very fast rate, unless he was just bluffing me the first 3 days. It is a possibility in a new environment. But, the balance issue is definitely not a bluff and he is coming around on that issue very fast also.

I have put him on the fat supplement to help him put on some weight. It is an additional monthly cost, but not that much. I do feel that it is important to try it. His weight issue is a priority and must be addressed aggressively. The feed that he was on may be a good product, but it wasn't getting the job done. I'm not trying to put on weight overnight, but we must find something that will make him begin to gain. I have had excellent results with the fat supplement, so that is where I started.

Zach has been a very good student since he arrived. He enjoys working, his ears are up and he is very interested in what is being asked of him. We have been having a good time together. I am leaving for the All-Morgan Monday pm. Maybe you can try to visit sometime between Friday eve and Monday, early afternoon. I am anxious for you to see him. And in watching him work, interested in hearing how much has changed, what he was doing with you and what he is doing now. It gives me a greater insight to what he knows and if it just got misplaced; and what he has improved upon. Reason being that he has made such great improvements since the first day that I rode him, I would like a better idea of what is new and what is old. Mostly for my own curiosity, it won't change his program at all.

Happy 4th!
Sandy

Sandy's farm was situated on a long dirt driveway, with a big rambling farmhouse dappled by the shade of tall oak trees. When I pulled up and climbed out of the truck, Sandy stepped through the screen door and greeted me with a huge grin.

"I read your book!" Her voice raised to an exultant pitch until it cracked. She squeezed my arm enthusiastically. "I love it! I think every Morgan horse owner should have one of these."

I hesitated. "Do you really think so?"

"Absolutely! I am going to make sure that everyone I know gets one. Do you have any? I'll sell them for you!"

"I have some in my truck."

"Great! Leave me six of them! No, leave me twelve!"

Zach was standing in his stall with his head hanging over the Dutch door, his ears pointed mildly in my direction. He nickered a soft greeting when I walked up.

"Hi!" I said, rubbing my hand across his soft muzzle and scratching the small white star on his forehead. He licked my arm in greeting, large long strokes with his wet tongue, like a dog.

Sandy stepped into the stall with a halter and put it on him. She led him out, his tall rangy bones rippling beneath his red coat, warm in the sunlight. She tied him to a post and said, "He's learning about this post. For some reason when I move my arm a certain way, it scares him."

"He does get scared of things," I said.

"Well, I just keep doing things over and over until he's used to them. I don't baby him. It takes him awhile but eventually he gets it. He's just not very sure of himself."

She saddled him up and then led him into her arena. She climbed aboard, her tiny figure straight and confident. Zach trotted off and she rode him for a bit.

"He looks great," I said. I watched his smooth stride, his easy reach, the relaxed way he dropped his head, and I could see that he was going to be fine with her.

August 2, 2001

Hi Nancy,

Zach is still training well. I have been riding him outside in the large field. It allows me to get his body alignment better. I can go straight for longer periods instead of always having to negotiate a corner after only a few strides. It has helped him a lot. He is beginning to pick up his correct leads out in the open field and getting better in the bridle. He has put on a lot of weight. He still has some to go but he is looking so much better. I'm leaving for Pennsylvania on Tuesday. I'll be riding him right through the weekend to make up for missed days while I'm gone. If you would like to come and see him, let me know. He is doing great!!

Sandy

September 1, 2001

Hi Nancy,

I have sold all of your books and need more. I have been spreading the word about Zach, yet no takers. He is still doing good. He has progressed nicely. Steps up, stops and walks over the bridge. Carries a feed sack of pop cans, sidepasses over the poles (with a little work), he is in the bridle completely at the walk and jog. We are working at the lope. He is getting better about his lead departures and has quieted down a lot. We have been working good together.

We still have about two weeks left to decide what to do with him. So, there is still time to put out an ad for him, if you want. I had an ad posted at the Buckeye show and spoke to quite a few people at the show, but still no real interest. I will still keep making contacts. Take care.

Sandy

When I visited Zach just a few weeks later, he didn't look the same at all. He was glossy and sleek with a layer of fat over his bones. His shoulders and rump were nicely rounded with muscle and his skin shone with good health. He appeared calm and happy.

"Sandy, I can't believe the difference just a few months with you has made."

"He's always had it in him."

I thought of Patty, how she had entrusted me with Buzz and L.B. "You know, I wonder if you would consider just taking him. I'll give him to you. I can't get him sold but maybe you can."

"Well, under normal circumstances I wouldn't do that. But this boy is really special. He needs someone gentle, and it might take time."

"Time is something I can't afford right now. I'm going through a divorce."

Her face sobered. "I thought it might be something like that. I'm sorry. I understand."

"I want to concentrate on promoting my book."

"Good for you! That is a great idea."

"If I gave you Zach, would you be willing to take him? Find him the right home?"

"Yes, I will take him."

I heaved a big breath of gratitude and relief. I helped her brush Zach as he stood in his stall, relaxing with his eyes half-closed.

"You can ride him!" Sandy said. She put a Western saddle on him, with a thick pad beneath, and led him out toward the arena. I followed her.

"Hold on to him for a minute," she said. I took the reins and Sandy walked over to slide the arena door open. As she walked away, Zach turned his head all the way around, away from me, and wistfully watched her go.

Chapter Twenty-One

*"We dare not forget that we are the heirs
of that first revolution."*
~ John F. Kennedy

Clifford had been invited as a special guest to Field Days in September at beautiful Merriehill Farm in Marengo, Illinois: Merriehill, with the white board fences, the huge brick buildings, the estate of famous glossy show Morgans. I was thrilled to be invited, but I decided that Clifford was too fat to be a special guest, and I had better start riding him every day.

On a beautiful early September morning, I rode Clifford on the dirt roads around the farm. Trotting down the road with the dogs, heading back home, I spotted a jogger a distance ahead of us. He was a thin, wiry young Mexican whom I assumed lived with the migrant workers on the big farm across the way from me. . He kept glancing nervously over his shoulder at us, and I realized he was worried about Cajun, now a big and intimidating shepherd.

"He's friendly!" I called. I had Clifford in a brisk trot, but we weren't gaining on the kid that fast. I couldn't believe it. He was really moving.

Finally, we caught up to him, and I said, "Man! You are working my horse's tail off!"

He looked over and grinned. He pointed to his shirt, which said, "U.S. Marines".

"I just finished boot camp," he said.

"Come on, Clifford! This kid is embarrassing you!"

He laughed. "What's his name again?"

"Clifford. He's named after my uncle."

"That's a nice name."

"Thanks! Boot camp, huh? Where are you going to be stationed?"

"I'm shipping out to Orlando, Florida next week. I'll be there three and a half years."

"Well, it's a good time of year to be heading that way. It will be cold here soon. Good luck to you!" I turned Clifford up the driveway.

"Thank you, ma'am." He continued on his way, never breaking stride, and didn't even seem short of breath.

I told Kimmy that night about the amazing Mexican Running Man, who held an entire conversation with me, all the while keeping pace with my trotting horse.

Five days later, the World Trade Center towers in New York City fell to the horrific terrorist attack now known as 9-11. Our country was at war.

The Mid-States Morgan Horse Club, who sponsored Field Days, decided to go ahead with the event even though it was to be held that weekend. I was shaken by the events as everyone was, but I agreed with the philosophy of moving on.

I had a new two-horse trailer, purchased just before the divorce. It was actually a used model with not very many miles on it. I had wanted a lighter weight aluminum one, but this one had been too good a deal to pass up. It was bright red in color. The hitch was a little different than I was used to, and it took me a little longer to get the truck backed up just right. But finally I got Clifford loaded and begin the long haul around Lake Michigan.

I had invited my friend Jennifer to go with me. The trip to Merriehill required a drive through Chicago, and I had forgotten about the hour time difference. We wound up driving in rush hour traffic. Every time another vehicle cut in front of us – which happened often – Jennifer would scream at them. It didn't seem to matter that the windows were rolled up and the other drivers couldn't hear her.

"MOVE, YOU IDIOT!" she screeched, lunging forward in her seat, as a battered Cadillac careened across the lanes. "USE YOUR ACCELERATOR!" she bawled at a pickup that inched its way down the road.

As the miles went on, there didn't seem to be any gas stations that were easily accessible, especially for a vehicle with a trailer.

"Don't they believe in rest areas around here?" Jennifer wailed. "Apparently commuters in Chicago have enormous bladders. Or permanent catheters."

We just kept driving, bumper to bumper, trying to avoid the potholes.

Driving past O'Hare International Airport was a sobering experience, as there was no activity. It was strange to see all the planes that hunkered silently on the flat concrete field, with none taking off or landing, no traffic hurtling toward the exit ramp and no vapor trails in the sky.

Finally, we pulled in the driveway of the Illinois woman who had offered a stall for Clifford during our stay. Chris Mothkovich greeted us with a brilliant smile and showed us the roomy stall she had all ready for Clifford. "You can just leave your trailer here," she offered. "Why should you have to haul it around?"

After Clifford was settled in, happily munching hay, and the trailer unloaded, we waved goodbye and went to find our motel room. Ten hours after leaving home, we finally trudged into the room. Throwing my bags down, I went to the sink and turned on the tap. But instead of water, out of the tap, with an asthmatic wheeze, came a torrent of icy brown sludge.

"NO!" Jennifer cried. "It can't be TRUE! Someone is playing an evil JOKE on us!"

She darted into the bathroom and turned on the shower. It coughed and then spewed out the same lumpy substance.

"Maybe it just needs to run for awhile," I said hopefully. I sat down on the bed.

"I'm going to cry!" Jennifer whimpered, leaning against the wall.

I picked up the phone and dialed the front desk. "Uh, we have a little problem here with the water."

"Oh, didn't we tell you? Our pipes are being redone in the morning. We've been having some plumbing issues. You can leave but if you stay, the plumbing will be fixed by morning. We'll offer fifty percent off your bill."

"I can't go any farther. I just can't!" Jennifer wailed, flinging herself on the bed.

We stayed that night without showering, only to find conditions the same the next morning. We went out to find another hotel.

"I can't believe they charged you fifty percent!" Jennifer said. "I wouldn't have paid a DIME for that place, not a DIME!"

We were scheduled to meet Chris for lunch that day. By the time we had showered and changed, Jennifer was in better spirits, especially at the prospect of a meal. We walked into the restaurant and Chris waved to us from a table by the window.

"I want to take you trail riding today," Chris said. "Jennifer, you can come too!"

"Ummm, thanks anyway, but I have a date with a Borders Bookstore," Jennifer mumbled.

That afternoon, Chris and I enjoyed a long trail ride among the beautiful golden leaves and twisted limbs of the trees at Oak Ridge Forest Preserve. I rode Clifford and Chris was aboard her beloved Morgan gelding, Gospel. Her conversation was lively and funny. As we rode along, the path ahead cut through a field of thick brush as high as Clifford's head. We were riding single file along this path, with Clifford leading, when suddenly a deer jumped right in front of us, flashing its white tail and leaping away again into the brush. Clifford shied violently, depositing me on the ground.

"Are you okay?" Chris said. Suddenly realizing I was laughing, she said, "What's so funny?"

"I haven't been dumped in a couple of years, but it just stands to reason it would happen on this trip! It's just the way things seem to be going!"

Clifford stood waiting and I climbed back on, then we resumed our ride.

I couldn't go through Illinois without visiting Clifford's breeder, Sharon Harper, and her beautiful horses.

Sharon met me at our hotel room and offered to guide me on the long hour drive to her farm in Forreston. She got in the truck with me. Jennifer, without one word of complaint, squeezed into the back seat.

All the way to the farm, Sharon and I talked about horses. She rattled off pedigrees and told stories of old Morgans from the past: the famous red chestnut, Pecos, who had passed his orange color through the generations and finally ending with Clifford. Upwey Ben Don, the bay stallion who infused many pedigrees with his type and tractable disposition. Elm Hill Charter Oak, whose owner, artist Jeanne Mellin Herrick, had found living in an obscure backyard and gone on to become a formidable park stallion with a tail that dragged the ground twelve feet.

We reached the farm, and as expected, Sharon presented a herd of typey, high-stepping Morgans with beautiful heads and snorty attitudes. Every single one of them was as kind and gentle as can be. There were old friends I hadn't seen in years: the stallion Kerry Freedom, so very like his sire Aries B; Kerry Hallelujah, the doe-eyed mare and dam of my own Trudy; Kerry Ariel, the big Morgan mare with the Friesian mane; Tara's Cotillion, still going strong at twenty two years of age.... And some new ones! Kerry Diva, a gentle bay weanling who lived up to her name; Kerry Free To Be, known as "Toby", the tall bay yearling who so reminded me of Clifford with that devilish gleam in his eye.

But when Sharon stepped into the stall and led out Kerry Freestyle, my heart skipped a beat. Here was equine

perfection. A bay weanling colt with a small star on his face, he had a cresty neck and
a beautiful head held high with pride. He was out of the mare Kerry Hallelujah, so was a half brother to my Trudy. He stood about waist high, his legs delicate and straight with big knobby knees. His eye was large and kind. His head swung around playfully as he grabbed at my sleeve.

"Oh Sharon," I said. "He is the one!"

I ran to get my camera. I remembered seeing Trudy for the first time, and the affect she had had on me as she trotted by her dam's side. This colt was very special. I knew Sharon didn't make a habit of photographing her horses, so I thought this was something I could do for her.

As I reached the truck, Jennifer said, "Are we going now?"

"I've got to take pictures first."

"You are taking one's picture?"

"I'm going to take photos of all of them!"

"NO!" she said in a stage whisper, leaning toward me, but I had the camera and was off.

I spent the next couple of hours with Sharon grooming and clipping each Morgan, getting them ready for photographs. Jennifer was sulking, but I was in heaven.

The next morning it was time for the Merriehill show. We pulled in to Chris's house, backed up the truck and Chris's husband Russ was kind enough to hitch the trailer for us. I loaded Clifford, had the directions to Merriehill, and we were off.

Driving along a two-lane highway toward Marengo, I looked in the rearview mirror and was horrified to see the red trailer drifting toward the cornfield.

"Oh my God!"

"What's happening?" Jennifer asked.

"It's come unhitched! Look!"

I slowed down and felt the gentle bump of the trailer hitch as it banged against the tailgate. I knew it was attached by the chains. I eased the truck to a stop and got out. Traffic whizzed by me unconcernedly as I walked back to see the trailer with its arm jammed up against the truck's bumper. It had drifted off to the side, but the chains had towed it. I went to the back of the trailer and looked in on Clifford, who stood inside with a confused expression.

Jennifer came up. "What has happened?"

"The pin wasn't inserted. The hitch was just resting on the ball and attached by those chains. It bounced off but the chains kept the trailer attached."

I couldn't unhook it as it was. The chains were completely taut. I had to back and pivot the truck to a point where they were loose enough to unhook. Meanwhile, traffic was zipping past us at an alarming rate.

"What is wrong with that guy? Doesn't he know how to hitch a trailer?" Jennifer said.

"It is my fault for not double checking." I made the third trip back from the driver's seat to see how else I could maneuver the truck.

Finally, the trailer was hitched correctly and we were back on the road. But my nerves were like tightening wires. What if the pin HAD been inserted, and had slipped out somehow? What if something was wrong with the hitch? If anything happened to Clifford… I kept looking in the rearview mirror at the trailer, making sure it was centered behind us.

At last we arrived at Merriehill, the big beautiful spread with brick pavement and white board fences. The chestnut stallion Merriehill Chicagoan acted as ambassador, whirling and trotting in his paddock by the stables.

Clifford was ushered into his own roomy, immaculate stall. My books were laid out on a table by the office, for people to flip through or purchase. We were treated like royalty.

Clifford was scheduled for two clicker demonstrations, one to be given that morning and one later in the day.

Jennifer approached me when Clifford was settled into his deluxe accommodations.

"I can't believe this!" she wailed. "I went into the kitchen to ask for water, and some tight-lipped spinster told me to USE THE HOSE!"

"Maybe she thought you were watering a horse," I suggested.

"Oh no. She knew what I meant. I'm beginning to think the entire state of Illinois is cursed! CURSED!"

She whirled and left the barn.

The Field Days event was held in a large grassy outdoor arena that had a track around the outside. A gaggle of Morgan horses were there, to present the various riding and driving disciplines. Spectators were treated to several different demonstrations. Exhibitors showed up dressed in patriotic garb, displaying loyalty to the country and acknowledging the current events. The day was sunny and bright, and spirits seemed high. When it was Clifford's turn, he performed his tricks flawlessly, only embarrassing me once when I turned him loose and he took off to the grassy part and started eagerly cropping the rich green turf.

"Guess I'd better start feeding him once in awhile," I muttered, and everyone laughed. But he allowed me to approach and grab his halter, and he good-naturedly performed the rest of his routine, and then we retired to enthused applause.

Jennifer rushed up to me as I led Clifford down the cobblestones toward the stable. "WHEN can we get out of this HELLHOLE?" she screeched.

I paused, looking around to see if anyone from the estate had heard her.

"He has one more demo, and then we can leave," I said.

"Thank God!"

Later that afternoon, the National Anthem was played as the black Morgan gelding, MNK Made to Play, carried a rider with a large United States flag around the arena. Someone had told me it was "Playboy's" first time carrying a flag, but he did it with style and grace. People removed their hats. There was a hush as this quiet demonstration took place. Some people wept softly. I couldn't think of a more appropriate way to make this gentle statement. The Morgan was, after all, America's first breed.

When the trailer was hitched and we were driving back that evening through Chicago, it was heartening to see the illuminated signs everywhere, "God Bless America", and the jumbo jets once again taking off and landing at O'Hare International Airport.

By then, it wasn't difficult to keep things in perspective.

Chapter Twenty-Two

*"A man wrapped up in himself
makes a very small bundle."*
~ *Benjamin Franklin*

Clifford's celebrity was spreading quickly around Michigan among the Morgan folk. Anne Wyland, who owned the lyrically named Ancan Morgan Farm, hosted an annual trail ride at her home that fall. She invited me to come and sign books. She lived in Davison, not far from the Genessee County Trails which wound for miles along the river and through the hardwoods surrounding it.

Eight Morgan owners showed up that day to ride. We walked and trotted along the leaf-scattered paths, enjoying the shimmering gold of seasoned oaks and enormous green pines. Anne liked to trot ahead on her mare, turning to point a camera at the rest of us as she rode. I laughed as I wondered aloud how the pictures were going to turn out.

Clifford was happy as always to be in the woods. He never hesitated to cross a stream or a bridge, and thanks to all our years on Drummond, would step willingly over downed trees as well.

Some of the others were not so confident. We crossed over one especially bushy tree that obstructed the path, and only one other horse followed. Then I heard Anne calling, "Wait you guys! We have to move this tree!"

We turned back. I hopped off Clifford and just let him go free. He simply stood there and watched with interest as Anne and I pulled the tree off the path. It was heavy. I looked up at him and gasped, "You know, if you were anything like your ancestor, the first Morgan, you would be doing this for us!"

When I spoke to him he walked up to me.

"What a good boy he is!" someone said. But I knew that, after all the years of freedom up on Drummond, he would never leave me stranded.

We mounted again, and finished our ride in a satisfying three hours. When we got back to Anne's we found a spread of Kentucky Fried Chicken provided by the Michigan Justin Morgan Horse Association, who had sponsored the ride. Others had brought potato salad and various desserts. We untacked our horses and got them settled in trailers or tied, and then sat down and dug in. It was a wonderful day.

I signed a stack of books for everyone. We visited with Anne's beautiful old stallion, Fiddler's Blackriver, and his herd of mares and foals. Then, the group began to disperse. I walked toward the trailer where Clifford stood waiting with his head hanging out through the manger door. His eyes were half-closed.

I was feeling quite at peace with the world, and quite satisfied with myself. People raved about this book. Clifford was going to be famous. Maybe I would actually sell a lot of them! Maybe I had found my niche! I couldn't help beaming. It was so nice to be recognized.

A lady paused ahead of me and turned back. She held up my book, which said "CLIFFORD" in big white letters. She gestured with it toward my trailer, where the dozing Clifford stood, as she asked, "What is your horse's name, again?"

Chapter Twenty-Three

"And God took a handful of southerly wind, blew His breath upon it, and created the horse."
~ Bedouin legend

"Are all Morgans like him?"

I heard the question many times at the North American Horse Spectacular in Novi that November weekend. Thousands attended this event yearly, which hosts vendors of Equine Everything; from horse trailers to stalls to tack to stuffed toys; training and riding demos, and of course the Parade of Breeds.

Electricity was in the air. The Michigan Justin Morgan Horse Association had a stall ready for Clifford, hock-deep in shavings. The aisle was lined with indoor-outdoor carpet, and row after row of portable stalls housed horses of every breed imaginable: Friesians, Clydesdales, tiny miniature horses, speckled Appaloosas. On the front of Clifford's stall was a blue and grey curtain with the club's logo on it, a lovely drawing of a Morgan horse by Jeanne Mellin Herrick.

Clifford was in his element. His ears were up, his eyes snapping with excitement. He clearly loved the attention. Crowds would pause in front of his stall to pet him through the bars and offer him carrots, which vendors were selling for 25 cents a bag.

The vendors were intoxicating. There were so many things available to tempt the horse owner – books, videos, and booth after booth of tack and grooming supplies. MJMHA had set up a table for me near Clifford's stall, where I could sell books. They also had a booth in the vendor section right by the front door, with fliers and photos and information promoting the Morgan horse.

I sat near Clifford all that Friday evening and answered questions about Morgans. Our arena appearance was scheduled for Saturday morning, with the Parade of Breeds. Each breed was allotted three minutes in the arena.

As I stood in the stall the next morning brushing Clifford, one of the show coordinators came up and said, "Okay, you are next after the Thoroughbred. Get ready!"

I quickly slipped Clifford's purple halter on. As I opened the stall door, the woman walked down the aisle ahead of us saying, "Horse coming through! Clear the way! Horse coming through!"

Clifford stepped out of his stall with his head down and his ears up, and followed me eagerly through the crowd. I was carrying his orange cone in my left hand, trying to keep it out of his sight, and I dropped it by the arena gate. My friend Logan Hyatt of Marshfire Morgan Farm was a musician, and had supplied me with a cassette tape of the Charlie Brown theme in piano called, "Linus and Lucy". I was wearing my fanny pack and had it filled with treats. We were ready.

As the Thoroughbred left the ring, the gate swung open and I heard Logan's slow introduction in piano playing over the loudspeaker. I led Clifford through the soft sand of the area and stood him up, stretched in a show pose, while the announcer read the script I had prepared.

"The Morgan horse is an American breed that began in the 1700's with one stallion of unknown lineage. His name was Figure, and he belonged to a poor schoolteacher named Justin Morgan, who accepted the colt as payment when the owner couldn't pay cash.

"Figure is reputed to have been the size of a large pony, standing barely over 14 hands tall. But he could work in the Vermont forest all day skidding logs, and in the evenings go into town and win races. He raced Thoroughbreds, Arabians, and all kinds of horses and was never defeated. This plucky little bay horse quickly gained notoriety for his strength, versatility, and tractable disposition. But he became even more famous because of one outstanding quality: Nearly every foal Figure sired, no matter what mare he was bred to, was a carbon copy of himself!"

Logan's music was now escalating into the familiar lively theme. I unhooked the lead rope and Clifford was free. I swung the end of the rope over my head in a circle, mimicking a lasso, and he broke into a spirited trot. Around and around me he trotted, and I realized he was longeing instead of just running loose. That was fine with me. After he made a few passes, I dropped my arms, pointed at his chest and said, "Whoa."

He stopped immediately and stood there, exactly as I had taught him to do when he was a two-year-old.

The crowd went wild! I hadn't expected the enthusiastic applause.

The announcer went on, "Figure's wonderful tendency to reproduce himself is what created the Morgan breed. The early Morgans were small, muscled, with cobby bodies, cresty necks and pretty heads. The Morgan horse can be found behind virtually every American-bred horse known today: including Quarter Horses, Tennessee Walkers, and even the wild Mustangs.

"Known for its tractable disposition, the Morgan horse is famous for versatility as well, excelling in carriage driving and the many disciplines under saddle. Morgans can be seen all over the nation and in many situations: Herding cattle, on endurance and trail rides, pulling carriages, jumping, dressage, parades, Civil War reenacting, you name it, a Morgan can do it."

I stepped up next to Clifford's left side and signaled him to follow me. We did a free lead, with him staying at my right shoulder, walking in a circle around the area. I trotted, he trotted. I stopped, he stopped. I backed up and so did he.

The crowd was loving us. I was starting to feel pretty good about all this stuff I had taken for granted for so long. Clifford was happy just being clicked and earning his peppermints for a routine he knew so well.

"Representing this breed today is Kerry B Proud, a nine year old chestnut gelding also known as Clifford," the announcer said. "Clifford has been trained using operant conditioning, otherwise known as the clicker method, and can perform some tricks. He can be ridden either English or Western, is great on the trails and in parades. He can carry a rider of any age."

Now Clifford and I were doing our fancy park walk, simultaneously lifting first one knee, and then the other.

"Clifford has the typical Morgan personality: Outgoing, fearless, and insatiably curious. You can learn more about these wonderful horses at the Michigan Justin Morgan Horse Association's breed booth."

Knowing our time was almost up, I ran over to the gate and reached through for the cone. I turned around and almost bumped into Clifford, who was standing behind me waiting for the next cue. He saw the cone, and his head dropped immediately into the waiting position. I shook it a little, signaling him that I was going to toss it, then I flung it out into the arena.

He whirled and ran over to it, with his head rolling in playful circles. I started laughing. I couldn't believe what a ham he was! Then, with his usual flair for the dramatic, he stood over the cone and stared into space. The crowd was silent. Nobody moved.

"Pick it up!" I yelled.

He reached down, picked it up and came gunning back. A roar came up from the stands. People leaped to their feet. There was Clifford, head high, tail up, trotting toward me, bearing that orange cone like it was a prize. I was seeing it as if it was slow motion. I had chills.

He delivered it to my hand as always, earning his peppermint.

The announcer was chuckling now, but dutifully read the conclusion of the script. "We are proud to present the Morgan horse, a breed which embodies the spirit of this great country, which has developed through the 200 years in its bosom. The Morgan is a true American original."

I clipped the lead rope back on Clifford and led him from the arena. The crowd was still applauding.

I realized that the spirit of patriotism, the emotional times were part of what made Clifford's performance so special, and the crowd's reaction so enthusiastic. With the breed's fabric woven deeply into our history, the Morgan horse represented our country like no other.

When Clifford was returned to his stall, a crowd gathered around to see him up close. People were smiling, reaching out to touch him.

From that point on, I spent the rest of the weekend answering questions about Morgan horses and clicker training. Scorch helped me by demonstrating how the clicker worked, doing tricks in the aisle while people gathered around, and Clifford nickered indignantly from his stall.

After three long days at the Expo I was not surprised to see some horses getting burned out. They stood with their backs to the aisle, heads down, eyes half shut, willing themselves away from the noise and constant chirping beckons of passersby. Yet on Sunday afternoon, there stood Clifford, nose pressed between the bars, ears perked forward, eyes eagerly awaiting the next guest. His insatiable greed for attention had surpassed my expectations. He must have eaten twelve pounds of carrots as the day wore on, suffering the sticky fingers of small children and showing intense fascination with one little boy's plastic cowboy hat.

Perhaps the most touching moment of all was with the woman in the wheelchair who could not see over the stall door. Her hands were twisted against her chest and her head bent on one shoulder. She couldn't speak. The man pushing her was looking at Clifford. "Here we have a Morgan gelding," he told her. "He is chestnut with a white blaze, and lovely brown eyes."

I walked over and said, "Here, take a look."

I opened the door and the man wheeled her in. Clifford approached her immediately, and keeping his usually busy lips still, he bent over her, and ever so gently blew on her arms, hands, face. The lady murmured something and the man answered, "Yes, he is a nice horse. Thank you."

It occurred to me as he rolled her away, and I shut the stall door, to wonder how Clifford would know the appropriate thing to do -- and even more, how I knew that he would.

Chapter Twenty-Four

"A friend knows the song in my heart and sings it to me when my memory fails."
~Donna Roberts

Winter inevitably set in, putting an end to most of my outdoor activities, as well as my avid book promotion. Things at home became very quiet in a way that seemed sudden and unexpected.

Standing in the manure-filled stall, with my breath curling out in frosty puffs as I pushed the manure fork, I dejectedly glanced out at the pearly gray sky. Great. More snow. Clifford greedily stood with his head immersed in his feed bin and rattled his grain with emphasis.

"Move over," I said crossly, poking him with the fork.

He obliged, lifting one foot after another, and edged against the wall without ever raising his head.

It was a day that seemed overwhelming. I had just finished doing taxes and was worried about money, settling into life on my own, and I was missing Reva terribly. She had been gone six months and there was still an aching void. She wasn't there to help me carry buckets, to protect us, to keep the other dogs in line, indeed to keep Clifford in line.

Piper the Papillon too was gone at age twelve, only months after I'd lost Reva. The timing of their passing, in the midst of my divorce, seemed orchestrated to leave me feeling completely alone. I guessed I was supposed to be learning some kind of lesson, but I didn't feel any smarter.

I nudged the manure fork under another frozen lump and felt a tear sliding coldly down my cheeks. Clifford swung his head toward me, jaw working busily. His ears perked forward. He took a step away from the bucket and reached for the fork, grabbing the end of it and pulling.

"Let go!" I said, waving him away. I wiped my nose on my glove and continued scooping as I morosely thought of how an animal family was a temporary one. Clifford, I realized, was ten years old this year. Scorch was seven. Trudy was eight. Their days were numbered! All of them! I squeezed my eyes shut and sobbed.

When I opened my eyes, I saw the white diamond that adorns the end of Clifford's nose. It was two inches from my face.

"Will you stop!" I said, reaching out and pushing on his neck.

He lowered his head and began nibbling on my hand. The white diamond jumped as his muzzle busily worked, worked, worked on the fingers of my glove, feeling delicately for the loose ends and then pulling softly. He pulled the glove completely off my hand and moved away with it dangling from his mouth.

I stood still. "WHAT are you DOING?"

His head went up, up, up, pointing at the ceiling, with the glove flipping gaily as his eye rolled toward me. Then with a dramatic flip, he dropped it.

"Nice!" I said. "Throw it in the poop!"

He reached down, picked it up, stepped over to me, and presented it to me. As I took it, he stepped back and waited expectantly, with his tousled hair hanging in his eyes, blowing warm breath that turned to white clouds in the air.

"You are definitely loony tunes," I said, but by now I was laughing. He returned to his grain then, his mission accomplished.

Had I been thinking I was alone? I must have been crazy.

Chapter Twenty-Five

*"Everybody needs beauty as well as bread,
places to play in and pray in,
where nature may heal
and give strength to body and soul."*
~John Muir

"I've given permission for them to run an electric line through here," Dad said that summer, nodding toward the road that stretched through camp.

"What? Who is putting electricity in?"

"Rory O'Neal. He owns Clifford's Bay now."

I suddenly felt short of breath. Clifford's Bay, our playground, the beach where my great-grandfather had sailed in and first set foot on Drummond in 1880.

"Dad, why did you give them permission?"

"I didn't want to create hard feelings. Besides, they would just go across the road or around the property. This is progress and we can't stop it."

Drummond had seen a constant influx of development of late. The western shoreline, once a solid wall of cedars visible from across the St. Mary's River, now had scars harboring rows of identical condominiums. New homes and cabins and cottages were popping up everywhere, especially on the water's edge. Shore front land was at a premium, with prices shooting higher despite the lapsed economy. Our island, as we knew it, was no more.

But Clifford's Bay remained, a safe haven for the wild things that came down to drink in the night, to the suckers and salmon that spawned in the creek there. The sandy beach, one of the few on the rock-based island, spread clean and inviting to Lake Huron. The water lapped softly there, protected by the wide, shallow inlet.

Part of the land around the bay was owned by the state, but other parts of it were privately owned by one man who acted as steward of the land for years. He didn't do anything to change it. He had died that spring and left the property in care of his family, who had sold it to the developers.

I felt a surge of panic. I had to do something. I began contacting every state representative and organization I could think of who could help preserve this tiny sanctuary. I contacted the Department of Natural Resources, the Michigan Environmental Council, the Nature Conservancy and the Little Traverse Conservancy. I contacted Governor Granholm. I contacted the Drummond Island Historical Society with the suggestion that the place could be preserved as a historical landmark.

I received polite responses that all sounded something like, "Though Drummond Island sounds worthy of protection, we don't currently have the funding necessary to secure the lots."

It was too small a piece of property in too remote an area to be of much interest to larger groups. Months later, when I had exhausted all my resources, and the groups started referring me to people I had already contacted, I knew my fight was over.

I sent a final protest to the local paper, the Drummond Island Digest:

"Over the past nine summers I have been trailering my horses up to Drummond to spend time with Dad and ride in the woods. I like to ride down to Clifford's Bay in the evenings, when it's quiet and cool and the light is soft. The road to Clifford's Bay is narrow and crooked and riddled with rocks. After heavy rains it is often flooded in places. I like this inhospitable two-track, because it guarantees me a safe place to ride, since vehicles that can get down there generally don't go very fast. I can turn one horse loose while I ride the other, and let it run and play with the dogs.

"When we get close to the beach, the loose horse will gallop past me and run down to the shore to roll in the sand. Our approach is quiet and we often scare up a deer, or heron feeding on the shoreline. I've seen a hoard of terns dive-bombing a school of minnows in the center of the bay, heard loons calling, and watched the evening light play on a wealth of wildflowers such as iris, touch-me-nots, bluebells, and many more.

"The air is primeval. It isn't difficult to imagine scenes from the past: Wolves drinking from the creek, native Americans teaching their children to fish, George Warren Bailey's boat floating silently into the bay like a big bird. There is immense comfort in knowing that the place has remained virtually unchanged for thousands of years.

"This summer, when I go back, I will take a good look and hope to remember things as they have been. In a matter of months, what is the wink of an eye in the eons of Drummond's lifetime, Clifford's Bay will change. What to some is priceless, to others has been deemed worth six hundred dollars a foot. Bulldozers will come, the ancient cedars ripped out, and the road "improved" so an electric line can be put in.

"It is a scene not unfamiliar to Island natives – wild alcoves they have treasured since childhood now violated with the pounding of hammers and chain saws and orange signs that say "PRIVATE", as those who can pay six hundred dollars a foot come from miles to find a place to Get Away. They will leave their favorite TV shows so they can come north to tear down trees and put up condominiums and watch their favorite TV shows here.

"I will take a good look, and be grateful that for the first half of my life I knew a place like Clifford's Bay. I will take a good look, and in years to come I will tell people of an American beach where it was once safe to let horses run free."

Chapter Twenty-Six

``All change is not growth,
as all movement is not forward."
~ Ellen Glasgow

It was a long time before I finally was able to laugh about it, but I later joked that Morgans seem to do better when broiled, not baked. I had tried to cook both of mine that year when I headed north on a ninety degree day, hauling my new red steel two-horse trailer.

An hour into the trip, I pulled over to check on Clifford and Trudy, finding them both in a sweat and breathing hard. My cousin, who was following me, suggested, "Why don't we just pop these doors off?"

He reached up and easily lifted the tops of the trailer doors off their hinges, which immediately opened the interior to more circulation.

"I -- I didn't even know you could remove those!" I'd had the small side windows open, but in that heat it was insufficient. The poor horses were unloaded and we led them around the service station, their skin wet, nostrils flaring, eyes bright with feverish anxiety, looking around the new surroundings and guzzling water as it was offered.

I felt like the worst clod imaginable. If Clifford and Trudy had been human children, Social Services would certainly have come swooping down and borne them both away, just like the Winged Monkeys in the Wizard of Oz.

To my touched and grateful incredulity, both of the little Morgans climbed back into the trailer with no hesitation when they were asked. We drove the remaining hours with no further incidents, making frequent stops and crawling along at a rate far below the speed limit.

Trudy, being the Good Mare as always, never did have a problem. She still loaded, unloaded and handled each trip with aplomb. But Clifford did not forget this scary time, in this new trailer that had made him so uncomfortable, and he developed a habit of kicking the wall. He would lean into the partition, raise his left hind leg, and kick. Each kick ended with him stepping on the other foot and knocking a chunk of skin right above his coronary band, the sensitive area above his hoof. He would come out of the trailer with his right foot bloodied.

I loaded them both, every day, at camp. I fed them grain in the trailer, and soon they would load anxiously at mealtime. However, every time I tried to move the trailer, Clifford would commence his kicking habit. I started making him wear bell boots, which prevented injury but not the kicking.

I was dreading the trip back south. I finally could put it off no longer; the bear hunters were frequenting Drummond Island and deer season was approaching. So one October day, I loaded them again and began the long trip back downstate. Clifford was nervous, but handled it okay. He kicked every time we stopped, but did accept treats that I offered and enjoyed standing with his head out his window during our driving breaks.

But finally, pulling up into our driveway, it must have just been too much for him and he collapsed, crashing to the floor, with the tie rope holding his nose aloft. It was dark out, and I could not see him, but I heard him grunting in panicked desperation.

I opened the door and managed to get him unhooked. He immediately stood up and backed out, but he limped as he stepped across the driveway.

I led him into the garage and looked at his right hind leg, not surprised to see it covered with bloody cuts and scrapes. I hosed him off, and applied some salve. He was walking on it but obviously uncomfortable. It did not, however, affect his appetite. He and Trudy had new grass on a pasture that had been empty all summer, so they barely lifted their heads all night. By that time, they were a lot less stressed than I was.

Obviously, he was going to have to travel again at some point. But for the rest of that year, the flaming red trailer hunkered by the garage like a chore that was only half finished.

Chapter Twenty-Seven

"Let your friends be the friends of your deliberate choice."
~ Anonymous

The neighbor's house down the hill was for sale, and one day a potential buyer rang the doorbell and introduced himself. He came in with the realtor and we chatted for awhile about things like snow clearing and trash pickup. The realtor was standing near the window and she turned suddenly and said, "Your horses know you have company."

"Oh?"

She gestured toward the window. "That one with the white stripe is looking right in here."

I heard an unfamiliar equine voice squealing one night in November, and then some pounding hoofs. The ruckus was coming from my backyard. I ran outside, to find Clifford and Trudy standing quietly inside the fence, but there were tracks in the snow all over my backyard. No other horses appeared out of the darkness.

I led Clifford and Trudy into the barn and secured them in stalls. I didn't want them getting excited by loose horses and going through the fence. I filled a grain can and shook it, hoping that would attract the fugitive, but nothing happened. I went inside and called the police to report a loose horse. I hoped that the animal wouldn't hurt itself or run out on any roads, but I thought that for the time being, I had done all I could.

I woke up the next morning to find a tall dapple-gray mare standing out by my barn. She was conferring with Clifford and Trudy, who she could see looking out through their Dutch doors. She was jittery, her hair plastered down with dried sweat. But when I spoke to her, she came right up to me. She was wearing a halter, so I took it, led her inside and put her in the empty stall. She drained an entire bucket of water and then wanted more. I gave her a little grain, which she devoured gratefully.

I knew she belonged to Al, my new neighbor down the hill. He had acquired three horses shortly after moving in, and had put up a one-strand wire around an acre. His other two mares were still at home. I didn't know him well, but realized I should have thought to call him the night before.

I walked all around my fenceline, checking to see if she had broken through anywhere. The fence was fine, but her tracks were everywhere.

I walked through my field down to his house, went up the steps and knocked on the door. I heard something inside, but no one came. I waited a few minutes and then came back home.

Clifford nickered to me gently as I walked into the barn. I went into his stall, opened his door and let him outside, and he immediately went to the new mare's stall to visit with her over the Dutch door. He grabbed her halter in his teeth and attempted to pull it off. I let Trudy out then, and the three of them stood together blowing noses softly.

I gave the mare another bucket of water, which she guzzled eagerly. I threw them all some hay and then went back to the house, leaving the mare in the stall with the top Dutch door open.

I made two more trips to Al's house that day, and as evening fell I pinned a note to his door with my phone number. The mare had stood all day in the stall, and was still consuming lots of water. She had quieted though, and was more content now. Clifford and Trudy came in for the night and I left them in the barn, munching hay.

Finally, the next day, Al came to get his mare. "Her name is Shila. She's five years old. Not broke yet. She's an Arabian – Saddlebred cross."

"She is beautiful!" I said. And she was. She was tall, with a wide chest and straight legs and a warm rosy tinge to her dappled white coat. Her ears were tipped with black, and her eyes large and dark and intelligent. "How did she get loose last night?"

"She went through my fence."

"It's electric, right?"

"No. Just a wire."

That explained it. His other two horses were older and more seasoned, knowing enough to respect a wire boundary, that it might snap them unpleasantly if they touched it. But Shila was young and full of energy. She had tested the fence, and it wasn't enough to keep her in.

When Al stepped to the stall door with a lead rope, Shila rolled her eyes nervously, then turned and leaned out the window, bellering to Clifford. Al hesitated. "I haven't had horses very long," he confessed.

"Here, I'll do it." I took the rope and walked in, and Shila allowed me to clip it on her. I handed the rope to Al. He led her out the door and she went willingly enough, but kept swiveling her head around to look back at my horses.

Less than an hour later, I came home with groceries, and she was back. When I went out to the barn, she led me to the door and looked back expectantly.

And so it went. She came back two more times that day. The last time she came back, Al called me up and said, "You know, I am putting a charger in, but I can't do it right now. Could you keep her for a week?"

"Okay, but you'll have to bring some hay, because there is a shortage this winter and I've only enough to feed my two."

"I don't want you to give her any food or water," he said.

"What?" I didn't think I was hearing him right.

"I don't want her to feel welcome there."

"Al, she has to have food and water. Horses need to have a lot of hay and water, every day. They need to keep eating and drinking and moving -- it's really important to keep their system working or they will colic and die."

"Really? I didn't know that."

He brought one bale – enough to feed her for barely two days. I decided that my Morgans were fat enough to ration the rest with complete feed, which contained all the nutrients they needed. In the meantime I thought Shila a bit thin, so I gave her Purina Senior, too. She was edgy in the cross ties, so I worked with her a little, and found her to be high-strung but good-natured. I was hesitant to turn her out with Clifford and Trudy, because she was much taller than they were, and seemed perpetually squealy. So, I kept her by herself in a separate field, though she visited with them over the fence. She was content to paw through the snow for remnants of grass, and come in at night with my two.

After that week, Al came and took her home, and she still didn't stay there. From that point on the mare came every day. Some days he did come and take her back, some days he didn't bother.

"If she keeps this up, I will have to sell her," he said.

"Do you want me to see if I can find her a home?"

"I don't want to sell her. I love her."

When he did take her home, he tied her to a post and gave her no food or water as punishment. One day when she came over, her front legs were tied together with a nylon lead rope. The knots were tight on her coronary band, the sensitive area above the hoof, and I immediately cut them off.

I called him then and told him that he really needed to work on his fence, or do something with the mare. I said it was not good to tie her feet together. "If you want to give her away, I will take her. But I can't give you any money for her."

He came then, just before Christmas, and led her home again. I cried as I watched her look back over her shoulder and whinny to Clifford. Somehow, Al managed to keep her there this time, and for the next few days, every time I stepped outside she would call to me.

I was in a quandary. The mare was obviously neglected, but if I filed a formal complaint with the Humane Society, he would receive, at best, a warning. The mare was being fed at times, and he had constructed a three-sided shelter for the horses. I didn't think his abuse was clear enough to warrant any action. Furthermore, if I complained, I would be alienating myself from him, and then unable to help Shila.

I wrote to my friends, the Morgan list on the Internet, and received all kinds of advice – everything from calling the police, to attempting to educate Al, to slapping him silly!

Then, I received a call from Susan Wagner of Equine Advocates in New York.

Equine Advocates is a non-profit organization dedicated to educating the public about the abuse of horses. Fortunately for me, and for Shila, the mare, they do take on some rescue cases as well.

"We're not in the business of buying horses," she said. "We just couldn't afford to save them all that way. But we need to do something for this mare."

Throughout that day we negotiated with Al. He was adamant about her sale price despite my explanation that the mare would need a coggins test, and there would be transport fees to get her to New York. Nevertheless, a price was agreed upon, and Shila was sold to Equine Advocates. I would foster her until she could be transported to New York. She would be adopted to a good home, but would remain under the wing of Equine Advocates throughout her life. Shila would never be sold at auction. If she ever had to change ownership again, it would be through Equine Advocates.

The last time Al had taken Shila from my property, he moved her to a neighbor's place down the road. These neighbors, the Smiths, had horses and had agreed to keep her with theirs. Susan requested that Shila be brought back to my house as soon as possible.

Al agreed to go get her and bring her over.

It was just getting dark when I heard unfamiliar squealing out back. I put my coat on and went out to see what I could do to help Al.

To my surprise, down by the barn were not only Shila, but two other horses as well. Both were geldings, a white Arabian and a Paint. All three were milling around loose, blowing steam into the air and kicking clods of snow. Al was nowhere in sight.

"What is going on out here?" I said.

Shila immediately turned and came up to me. She was wearing a halter, so I took it and led her into the barn. I put her in the empty stall. The other two horses followed me into the barn as well, their hoofs clattering and clopping up the aisle behind me.

Just as I was turning to reach for a lead rope, the fat Arabian spun and galloped outside, as two out-of-breath and very excited women ran toward us. Alarmed, the Paint flung his head up and broke for the door.

"Rocky, no! NO!" the woman shouted. She slid the door shut, trapping him inside.

"Is this someone you know?" I asked calmly.

"These are our horses!" Rocky the Paint was quickly cornered and a halter put on him. The woman explained that Al had left the pasture gate wide open when her husband went out to catch the mare. Shila, seizing the opportunity, bolted through the open gate and came flying down the road, taking the Smith horses with her.... Straight back to my house!

After a little more excitement, the Smiths caught their Arabian and led their two runaways up the driveway. I looked at Shila, who now watched me from her stall with a contented and innocent expression.

"Well, you must think this place is just all that! Sure! Tell your friends!" I dumped a scoop of grain into her bin and snapped off the light. But I am sure she could hear me laughing all the way back to the house.

Chapter Twenty-Eight

"The heart has eyes which the brain knows nothing of."
~ Charles H. Perkhurst

As the winter wore on, I was having more and more thoughts of spring and the inevitable trailer trips, and Clifford's new phobia.

My friends Lyn and Harry Alban suggested that I try talking with an animal communicator, to find out exactly what it was about the trailer that was bothering Clifford so much.

I was dubious at best. I didn't believe in psychics or things like that.

Kimmy did. "Try it! It's just like that book I sent you by Sylvia Browne! Remember? If we have past lives, why can't animals? Maybe that trailer reminds Clifford of something that happened to him in a past life!"

"That makes it sound even crazier," I said.

"It sounds crazy but you just never know. There are some things that just can't be explained."

I had a flashback to Reva's experience with Grandma's ghost. "That's true."

"And it can't hurt. What have you got to lose?"

"I'll give it a shot." How else was I going to find out what may be going through the noggin of Clifford -- an area where only the most valiant of souls would dare to tread?

The Albans had referred me to Mary Long, a lady who did readings over the phone. It seemed pretty simple. All I had to do was call her, and she would "listen" to Clifford, via a phone conversation with me.

Her voice was kind and surprisingly normal. I had half expected her to sound scratchy or start cackling.

"I can schedule you for two o'clock tomorrow," she said. "The conversation will last half an hour. Who do you want me to talk with?"

"My horse," I said. It was all I told her. I decided to give her as little information as possible, just to see what she would come up with. I was skeptical, but starting to get really excited about this. It was going to be fun and interesting, at the very least.

Just before we hung up, she said, "Oh, and your horse has already butted in and told me, 'I have very nice ears.'"

My reaction was to laugh and not say anything, but this wouldn't surprise me for two reasons: 1) Clifford butting in to anything is not an unusual event and 2) He really does have beautiful ears, and in fact I'd been thinking about them just the night before, because I was looking through some press release photos and admiring how well he used them for the camera.

Still, it seemed a safe enough thing for her to say. What horse doesn't have nice ears?

The next day at two o'clock sharp, I made the call.

"First tell me some things about your horse. What is his name, what does he look like, and how old is he?"

"He's Clifford. He's a red chestnut with a white blaze. He's eleven years old."

The first thing she said after I described him was, "He is jealous of a dark-colored mare. Do you have a dark-colored mare around there anywhere?"

This startled me, of course. "Yes, that would be his half sister, Trudy."

(My skeptical voice said: Maybe she's read the book.)

"Does she get more attention?"

"In a way. I hug her more, and certainly brag her up more. She's everyone's darling."

"This really bothers Clifford! Is there anything you can say to raise his self-esteem?"

(Skeptical voice: CLIFFORD with low self-esteem?!)

"Well," I said, "Clifford is certainly one of the most special creatures in my life. He's one of a kind."

"Oh, that's great!" she said. "I'm telling him that. Now what did you want to talk about?"

"I need to talk about his new trailer phobia. The trailer got very hot last summer and since then he's been having panic attacks inside it." I described the situation, how the trailer was a new one and I hadn't known enough to remove the tops of the back doors.

She listened carefully and then responded. "He said the trailer got hot but not brutal. It was hard to breathe, though. Don't worry about the heat. Yes, the old trailer was better, but that's partly because he was used to it. Does he travel on the right?"

"No. He's always on the left."

"He wants to be on the right. I keep seeing him on the right. Is the hitch different on the new trailer?"

(Skeptical voice: Well, other horse people have suggested I switch sides too. But I hadn't tried it yet.)

I paused. "Yes, it is a different hitch."

"What's different about it?"

"There's a pin that slides through it. Once, we were on a long road trip out of state. I forgot to slide the pin and the trailer came loose, attached only by the chains, and was drifting down the road and banging into the back of the truck. That scared the crap out of me! And that was BEFORE I tried to cook him!"

She started laughing. "You're too hard on yourself."

A moment later, she added, "Clifford was scared by that too. He still wants to go with you, though. Where do you go?"

"We go up to the Upper Peninsula to an island. Drummond Island. We go north every summer and ride in the woods and on the shore."

She interjected, "He LOVES that! He loves it when you ride him in the water. He wishes you'd feel comfortable riding him with just a rope around his neck."

(Skeptical voice: I'll bet he does.)

"He really loves you and he thinks that you have that kind of connection. But now he is adding, 'Which is obviously never going to happen if Trudy is in the picture.'"

"What is with this attitude toward Trudy? She's his sister, they love each other! They've lived together for six years."

She said, "Well, I'm going to ask him if he will be all right to travel this year. When will you be trailering him next?"

"Thank you! Probably not until June."

"Who is the Mud Horse? Do you have a horse that likes to roll in the mud?"

"Um, that would be Trudy." Trudy, the dainty Lady and Pig. She wasn't happy unless she was completely covered in crud.

"He says, 'Is the Mud Horse going with us?'" She was laughing.

"Wow! I had no idea he felt this way. Perhaps they just aren't getting along at the moment."

"That could be."

She said that Clifford was, "quite an interesting boy" and that he felt like a stallion, with the energy and sensitive conscientious nature of a stallion. She said that he has a great work ethic, and that all Morgans do.

She asked, "What else do you do with him?"

"I'm a clicker trainer. Clifford does tricks and stuff. He's sort of an ambassador for the Morgan breed. He makes public appearances."

I didn't mention the book.

"Oh, that is great! He loves your clicker sessions. He likes the crowds, except for when they 'erupt'. I'm telling him applause is the way humans show appreciation."

Mary was very concerned with health and the horse's comfort. She went on for a while about how Clifford liked his tack to be clean. Then she said, "Clifford is a very sound horse. No aches or pains anywhere! You are managing him very well. And he has terrific feet! He says he has never foundered."

"Yes, that's right. He has good feet and he goes barefoot all the time."

Mary paused for a moment, and then said, "Do you have a calico cat? One that is grey and white and tan, a fluffy one?"

She was accurately describing Georgie, my old barn kitty. "Yes."

"Well, Clifford is complaining about this cat. He has some kind of problem with this cat."

George was elderly, and she had been retired from her barn duties and come into the house to live all winter.

"I don't know what the problem would be," I said. "Clifford hasn't seen her in months."

Mary hesitated. "He said the cat has more grey on it."

At this point she was losing me. Although definitely calico, George was more orange than grey.

We were running out of time, and I told Mary I had two more things to say to Clifford.

"Sure, go ahead."

"Clifford is very close to my Dad, and Dad is having surgery -- a hip replacement -- on Tuesday."

"What is your Dad's name?"

"Blaine."

"He wants to know if Blaine will have to be in a wheelchair."

My skeptical voice piped up, but then I remembered the lady at the 2001 Expo, who was wheeled right into his stall, and how gentle Clifford was with her. He made no faces at her. He sniffed her all over and didn't bite her or tug her clothes or anything.

"No," I said. "No wheelchair. He will walk with a walker and then later walk on his own."

"I'm telling him."

I hesitated. Here was the question I really needed to ask. "Does Clifford miss the old dog?"

"He did, but not now. He has grieved and moved on."

"He's never bonded with the other dogs the same way," I said.

"He says they are just dogs underfoot. They don't have the same personality. He says there is a grave."

(Skeptical voice: Old dog dies, of course there's a grave.)

"Yes, there is."

"Well, this might sound kind of silly, but if you can picture him standing by the grave, and using his hoof to scrape the ground and throw some dirt on it. Much as if you'd throw some dirt into a grave to say goodbye.

Animals are very good at accepting things. I think we can learn from them."

She said the last part so sweetly, I knew she could tell that this part of the conversation was for my benefit, not Clifford's.

She thanked me for calling and we hung up. It was a beautiful sunny day, and I walked the dogs down to the mailbox. On my way back, I noticed the same situation that had been going on for a week or so. Clifford was standing by himself, alone in the field, while Trudy fraternized with Shila in their own corner. Trudy was enamored of Shila. It was just now dawning on me that Clifford was left out. They were at least an acre apart, and even facing away from each other.

As I stood there looking at them, I thought back to last summer when I had ridden Clifford over to Reva's grave. She was buried in a quiet spot at the edge of the treeline, behind the sawmill. I had sat there on Clifford's back, trying to imagine what type of marker I could use for the spot. I remembered getting disgusted with Clifford because he wouldn't stand still while I looked around.

He was very busily pawing the ground with his front hoof.

I shrugged these things off, and went about my business. Two days later, I came home from the grocery store with some apples for the horses. I went out the back door, and looked out in the pasture. There, stepping carefully through the melting snow was a calico cat. It was fluffy with large grey patches, and smaller spots of tan and white. It crept quietly through the brown stubble, lifting each white foot high.

I stopped and just stood there. I had never seen this cat before. I looked over at the horses in the field. The two mares were busily grazing, but Clifford was standing very still. His head was high, his nostrils wide, his ears alert as he stared intently at the cat.

Chapter Twenty-Nine

"Fear is the highest fence."
~ Dudley Nichols

The wooden cart still leaned against the wall in a corner of my barn. I looked at it from time to time when I passed it to cut open a hay bale. It became a handy stand on which to pile baling twine. Other than that, I hadn't touched the "equestrian catapult", as my brother Dan referred to it.

I had always heard that the right thing to do was get back on the horse if you fell off. After the accident, I had never driven again. I knew at some point I would have to do it.

My friend Gina had referred me to her horses' trainer, Jacki Rodosalewicz. "She drives in shows, and she wins a lot," Gina had said. "But the best thing is that she's so good with the horses. I've got Missy there now. Come on down on Thursday and I'll introduce you when I go over there."

I thought that was a good idea. So later that week, Gina and I pulled in Jacki's driveway, graced with huge oaks. On the ancient red barn was a sign, "Little Bit O' Farm". It conjured a picture of Jacki as a cheerleader type, petite and blonde.

But the person who stepped out of the barn was far from what I expected. Jacki was a beautiful woman, square-shouldered with a long dark braid, and the angular features that spoke of some Native American blood.

Her stride exuded strength and confidence. She held out her hand to shake mine so forcefully that I was instantly intimidated. But I looked into her eyes – liquid and warm, an indefinable color, and I saw kindness there.

Gina's tall bay mare, Missy, was hitched and ready to drive, and I watched as Jacki drove her calmly around the arena, pulling a small wooden cart similar to my own. "She looks great!" Gina said.

"She's fine," Jacki said. "Nothing bothers her."

She pulled Missy to a stop in the center of the arena. Gina turned to me. "Do you want to go for a ride?"

I had a surprising flood of near panic, but I tried not to show it. My first thought was that the mare was too green, and my first ride should be with a more experienced horse. But Jacki sat there, smiling at me, and they both waited. It seemed like a long minute before I said yes.

I climbed into the cart. Jacki clucked to Missy and she stepped forward. As the cart lurched into motion, I had a queasy feeling. My hands were cold and the palms began to sweat. I rubbed them together. Jacki didn't look at me, she just casually chatted away about the mare. She was very nonchalant about the whole business. I hadn't told her about the accident, but I could tell that she knew.

She couldn't know the rest of it: That the next day a good friend had died. That my husband had dubbed me a "nothing", and then left to pursue a woman with no scars on her face. That my beloved dog had died. Logically, I was aware that these events were not connected to the accident, but somehow in my mind it was the catalyst for a string of disasters. Being in that rolling, jostling cart was causing me a flood of anxiety. I was envisioning myself pitching over the bar again.

Finally after a couple of passes around the arena, Jacki pulled Missy to a stop and I climbed out.

I smiled at Gina. "Well, there's one down, and one to go."

I was hoping my face wasn't too pale.

Two weeks later, I delivered Trudy to Jacki's farm. Trudy was settled into a roomy corner stall. I left her with some peppermints and said, "She'll be going up North for the Fourth of July, so I can't leave her but for a couple of months."

"That's okay," Jacki assured me. "It will be good for her to have a break then. We'll take it slow. I'll start out ground driving her, like she's never done it before, and then have her pull some weights before I start hitching her."

"She won't be any problem," I said. "She's always so good."

But I was wrong. When I went back a few days later to watch Jacki longe Trudy in harness, I was shocked at how Trudy behaved. Her head was flung high, her eyes rolled. She was sweating. Jacki stood in the middle of the arena and talked to her calmly, but Trudy was obviously ready to bolt. She trotted in a circle, her feet beating the ground with irregular thumps, her movements jerky and stiff.

I thought maybe she was waiting for a click, which I sometimes used when I longed her.

"Do you think she is confused?" I said as Jacki coaxed the mare to a halt and walked up to her.

"I think she's really scared."

"I don't get it. She wasn't hurt in the accident. She didn't drag or bash the cart behind her. She just broke free and ran off. She didn't get hurt at all."

"No, but you did." Jacki turned to me with a little smile. "And she knows it."

I paused. Trudy stood quietly now, glad to be finished, waiting with her head dropped and eyes half closed beneath the blinkers.

"Will she ever drive again?"

"I don't know. We'll see. Some horses never recover from things like this." Seeing my face, she quickly added, "But we'll try. We just won't rush her."

The first day Jacki hitched Trudy, I received a jubilant email that read, "We HOOKED!"

Nancy,

I hooked Trudy about an hour ago, my helper Tammi was here, barn nice & quiet, so we went for it. I long-lined her first, then we hooked her to the cart. Let it bump her first from both sides, then on to ground driving around the arena pulling the cart, Tammi had a longe line on her so she had something to attach to. Trudy did fine with all of that, so I sat in the cart & walked with Tammi still attached to her with the longe line. I made some noises from the cart, she was scared, but she did just fine with everything. So after all of that we stopped while we were all fine.

So far so good! I will let you know how we do the next time.

Jacki

I was there the second day Jacki hitched her. Trudy stood in cross ties in her stall, waiting. The harness was already on. Jacki came out, dressed in a helmet and something I later described as a "bullet proof vest". But I didn't joke at the time. She had young Tammi there helping, who got on one side of the mare and Jacki on the other. I stood holding Trudy's head while each woman grabbed a shaft and rolled the cart easily into place. Trudy stiffened when the shafts brushed her sides. I petted her, spoke to her softly, but her eyes rolled.

Jacki climbed in and took up the reins. I stepped back and Trudy immediately burst into a jerky trot. Jacki just let her go. She made two rapid circles around the arena. "Whoa," Jacki said. Trudy stopped and Jacki jumped out.

I sat down on a hay bale. I was a little dazed. It had happened so quickly. "That was a good run," Jacki said. "That was okay."

"If it doesn't work out, it doesn't work out," I said. "She doesn't have to do it."

"She needs more time," Jacki said. "This really scares her. She's okay with the ground driving now, she's used to me. But the cart scares her."

I didn't say it out loud, but I was thinking that I didn't blame Trudy. The cart scared me too.

Chapter Thirty

Piglet sidled up to Pooh from behind.
"Pooh!" he whispered.
"Yes, Piglet?"
"Nothing," said Piglet, taking Pooh's paw. "I just
wanted to be sure of you."
~ A.A. Milne

"Finally went to the doctor," Kimmy said. I heard her quick exhale, and knew she was smoking again.

"It's about time! What's the scoop?"

"First I want to tell you what happened on my way home from there."

"Tell me what the doctor said."

"Just listen!"

"Fine," I sighed.

Kimmy didn't drive; in fact she didn't even own a car, so she had to take a bus to see the doctor. "I was headed for the bus stop and this guy got shot in the throat right on the street corner. Right in front of me!"

"What? You're kidding!"

"I ran over to him and he was lying on the sidewalk, bleeding like crazy. I looked around and yelled and asked if anyone knew C.P.R. But they all just stood there and stared at him and this guy is bleeding out right before my eyes."

"Oh my god," I said. "What did you do?"

"What could I do? I got down and stuck my fingers in the hole!"

"Yuck!"

"Yeah. It stopped the bleeding but he wasn't breathing. I had to give him mouth to mouth."

"You did? Was he at least good looking?"

She laughed. "No, Bailey, he was a gang member. A street fighter type."

"But what about the guy with the gun? What happened to him?"

"He took off, of course," she snorted.

"Did anyone call the police?"

"Yeah but it took forever for the ambulance to get there. Seemed like forever, anyway. Then when they showed up they wanted me to just keep giving him C.P.R. while they got the stretcher ready and everything hooked up for him. I said, 'You have to take over!'"

"So they took over?"

"Yeah."

"Then what happened?"

"Then I threw up."

We both laughed.

"Is the guy okay?"

"Yeah, he'll live, they said."

"Oh my god, Kimmy! That is amazing! Do you know how incredible that is? You saved his life!" I was holding the phone to my ear, hopping on one foot in excitement.

"Yeah, now he can go back to his drive-bys and drug wars."

"Maybe not. Sometimes an experience like this will change a person. You've given him a second chance!"

"Yeah, maybe," she sighed, blowing more smoke, I knew.

"That's moxie, Kimmy! That's what I am always talking about! Moxie! You've got it!"

But her tone was suddenly quieter. "I have some news for you."

"What's that?"

She paused for a moment, taking a deep puff. Then she spoke.

"I have cirrhosis of the liver. I've got six months to live."

I sat down, suddenly. "Now that's not funny!"

"I'm not kidding, Darlin'. I wish I was."

My mind whirled. This could not be happening! It had to be a huge mistake. "Well, what about the liver's ability to regenerate itself? And what if you quit smoking?"

"It's too late."

Her voice was the same as ever, matter-of-fact. She wasn't emotional at all.

"Did you get a second opinion?"

"Don't need one."

I paused for a moment, digesting this, then asked, "Have you told your mom?"

"No! I'm not calling her! She'd be out here in two seconds flat. I don't need that and neither does she. I don't want anyone to know. Just you. And don't you dare tell her, either!"

"Okay."

"Promise!"

"Okay! I promise! But what about Gary? Does he know?"

"Yes, he knows and Makayla knows."

"Well, what did they say? What did they do?"

"Nothing. What can they say?"

"Do you want me to come out there?"

"No, don't do that. It wouldn't do either of us any good. It would only depress you to be here. I want to keep things as normal for Makayla as possible."

She still had half custody of her daughter.

"Kimmy, are you sure?"

"Yep." Another long breath, inhale, quick exhale. I envisioned the smoke shooting out of her mouth, curling upward past her red head, settling deeply into her charred lungs.

"Don't worry," she added. "When I get to the other side, I'll find Reva. I'll take care of her."

"No worries. She'll probably take care of you." I murmured. But the thought of Reva was a sharp jolt of reality, and now it was finally starting to hit me. After twenty-three years of friendship, of shared lives, from college days together, living together, and now our long distance sisterhood, there would be no more Kimmy. It seemed impossible. She was part of me, an unconscious presence, a staple. Like breathing.

"Kimmy, are you sure this isn't a mistake?"

She laughed. "Yeah, it's probably the doctor's screw-up. I'll live to be a hundred, that would be just my luck. One day we'll go and have that farm after all."

I knew she was lonely and miserable, and had been having health problems for some time. She wasn't working. She sat home and watched T.V., sharing the couch with her pit bull, Pooh Bear.

"Is there anything I can do for you?" I said.

"Nothing you haven't done already. Oh, be on the lookout for some packages. I'm putting some stuff together for you."

"You don't have to do that! Don't do that."

"I just want to get rid of some of the clutter around here," she said.

Perhaps unable to fully grasp the bigger picture, my mind was whirling with the small details of her life. Her couch, her books. Her stuffed animals. All my art work lining her walls. Her chubby and neurotic old dog.

"What about Pooh?"

"My mom will have to take her. She'll never get along with your dogs."

"I would take her. I'd work it out."

"I know you would. But I wouldn't do that to you. You are Makayla's godmother too, you know. If anything happens to Gary – "

"I would gladly take Makayla. I would treat her like my own. You know that."

She laughed. "Oh, you don't know what you're saying. She's a teenager now."

"It's okay."

"Okay, I will write it down. I have some stuff around here I need to go through. I want to send you some of my jewelry. I've got this little whale's tail charm you will really like. And I'm putting in my sapphire necklace and ring and some of my other things."

We were silent for a minute.

"I don't think I can handle this," I said.

"You know I will always be with you," she said softly.

It was perhaps merciful that I didn't realize there would be no six months, that there was in fact, no time left for Kimmy. A few short days later, her mother called me tearfully from California, saying that she was gone. She had gone into cardiac arrest, and being Kim, had called 911 herself and they had come and gotten her. But she had died in the hospital that morning.

It was a glittering cold April in Michigan, with ice that fell in sheets and coated the trees and power lines with a sharp clear edge. Every branch, every twig was hard and brittle. The earth was dark and frozen.

Chapter Thirty-One

"Despair is anger with no place to go."
~ *Mignon McLaughlin*

The island's call to me was stronger than ever that year. Shila had gone to her new home in New York, and Trudy had come home after spending two months with Jacki. "A long break will probably be good for her," Jacki had said. "We need to take it slowly anyway."

I loaded up my Morgans. Clifford was loaded on the right as Mary Long had suggested, and little Trudy on his left.

We traveled north through the lower Michigan cornfields, through Clare County where the pine trees began to take over the roadsides, and the oaks were thinning out. I stopped at several rest areas to check on Clifford. He was still standing, but shifting his weight hard to the right, leaning on the trailer wall. He was drenched with sweat and clearly not happy.

"It's okay," I told him. "Just hang in there."

We traveled farther north, past Grayling and Gaylord, where the hills became sandy and covered with ferns, and the forests were profuse with spruce and gleaming white birch.

We crossed the enormous Mackinac Bridge, the long expanse of highway that stretched over clean blue water. To the east, I saw the tiny white plume on the back of the white spot that was the shuttle to Mackinac Island. Freighters rested in the sparkling ridges of water, far below. I imagined the horses smelling the clean air, blowing into the trailer off the Straits.

Then there was the road to Drummond, the road thick with spruce and exploding with the strong scent of balsam, the curving highway along the sandy beaches of Les Cheneaux and DeTour. The sight of the Saint Marie's River and Drummond Island was immensely comforting to me.

When we finally pulled into camp and I lowered the ramp and opened the door, I saw that Clifford had been kicking again. His shipping boots were rumpled, but had protected him from cuts. Still, I was sure he must have bruised himself. Trudy backed out of the trailer, unhurt, looking around with excited anticipation, knowing where she was. Clifford backed out, trembling, unhappy, but looked around and brightened. I led him to the corral where both horses immediately dropped and rolled.

It was good to be back. The rocky shores loomed like towers of strength, and tree limbs spread like sheltering awnings. They seemed so solid and permanent.

It was a long summer of peace and sun. Clifford was in the parade again, but this year Dad couldn't ride him, since he was still recovering from surgery. I rode him myself, and this time people called his name as we passed. They knew him because of the book. It was exhilarating.

There was always a pervading sadness, but in the natural world it seemed easier to comprehend the circle of life. I watched the tiger lilies bloom, burst forth in brilliant orange, then gradually curl back toward the earth. The colors of summer eventually aged to the hearty gold and bronze of autumn.

But then one evening, walking out to Reva's Lake with the dogs, I noticed some heavy tire tracks and brush scattered over the road. I looked up and saw to my horror that the trees were chopped up, hacked to shreds, all along the roadside up to a height of fifteen feet.

I ran back to camp and got my truck. I wanted to follow these tracks. I imagined some idiot trying to bring a modular home down this road, something double wide that was mangling the limbs.

I followed the trail of brush, getting more and more upset as each corner revealed more trees being mutilated – white birches now with sickly pink gashes and stubs protruding like misplaced bones, cedars with limbs dangling and bark torn and hanging down in huge flaps.

I rounded the last corner and found a huge yellow brush hog with a rotary blade swinging skyward, tearing down the lower limbs of a large pine. The brush hog crawled along slowly. I pulled my truck around in front of it to block it, jumped out and yelled, "Stop!"

The man inside quickly shut off the engine and climbed out of the brush hog. I didn't recognize him. I approached him and he backed up a step. "Why are you killing these trees?" I demanded. "Who gave you permission to do this?"

"Well, I'm not killing them," he said.

"You think this isn't killing them?" I shrieked, gesturing to the grassy roadside, where lay a broken limb as large as my arm. I knew I was hysterical, but didn't care. "Who told you to do this? And why?"

"This is a new machine purchased by the DNR," he said politely. "I'm cleaning up the roads."

"This is cleaning up?" I looked at the pile of brush alongside each road, the amputated limbs and twisted branches.

"Oh don't worry," he smiled. "It will all be picked up when I finish. I won't leave a mess."

"I don't care about the mess!" I was literally hopping now. "Look at these trees. I've known these trees for ten years! I see them every day!"

"Well, see, they are a danger to the snowmobilers. So we're cutting back the limbs to leave an open space over the road. That way the snow load won't fall on anyone."

"That is the most ridiculous thing I have ever heard!"

He shrugged. "I'm just doing my job, ma'am."

"So where are you going next?"

"Well, I'll be doing all the snowmobile trails all over this area."

I'd been afraid he was going to say that. All my roads, my favorite places, were marked trails for snowmobilers.

Later, that fall, a trip down to Clifford's Bay revealed the same rape of the land. The cedars were mauled beyond recognition. And the man had not, as he'd said, "picked up." Dead branches were strewn everywhere. As I rode through the little hardwood, the spot where

Clifford had liked to play his game of hide-and-attack, I saw that the young maples were now only sticks protruding from the ground. I no longer had to bow my head to ride through, as there was no canopy of green anymore.

I couldn't stay on Drummond any longer. I loaded up the horses and we headed south.

Chapter Thirty-Two

*"Courage is not the absence of fear,
but rather the judgment that something else
is more important than fear."
~ Ambrose Redmoon*

That November, Clifford was scheduled to appear again for the North American Horse Spectacular. I was a little apprehensive about trailering even though Novi was only an hour away. I arranged for my friends Jim and Becky to help me. I'd follow behind the trailer and keep an eye on Clifford.

Clifford had been nervous on the long road trip back from Drummond, but he'd made it. It must have been the absence of Trudy that pushed him over the edge on the way to Novi. On I-96, as I was following the trailer toward Brighton, he disappeared from view. I immediately called Jim, who was driving the truck that hauled him, and told him to pull over. My worst fears were realized. Clifford had collapsed, his head hanging listlessly by the trailer tie, and had that glazed "I want to die!" look in his eye.

"CLIFFORD!" I tried to break through his fog with a familiar shriek. He finally struggled to his feet, but he was leaning on the partition and began kicking the wall with his left hind. After some discussion, we finally decided to get off the highway and take the Brighton exit until we figured out what to do.

We started off again and I dialed every person I could think of on my cell phone who might be able to help. I had absolutely no idea what to do. Even though I have owned horses for nine years, I still consider myself a novice in so many ways. I finally got ahold of my friend Gina Hyatt, who called Sue Hall. Sue owned a Morgan farm in South Lyon and after a short conversation, she said she would come right away with sedatives.

Clifford was down again when we pulled into the bank parking lot. I immediately unhooked him, but he was thrashing and somehow had wedged himself under the partition, with all four legs in the air. I dialed 911, and they said they would send the fire department. "Send them right away!" I pleaded. "This is an emergency!"

I had experienced few scarier things in my life. Clifford lay there on his back, hoofs curled up like a kangaroo, looking bloated and as if he'd lost the will to live. But when we pulled the partition out, he gamely struggled back to his feet and stood there quivering and breathing hard.

The fire department came, but by then he was up, so there wasn't anything they could do. Then Sue arrived. She went right into the trailer, speaking to him calmly. She told me, "Our show mare, Prize, was a scrambler too."

It was the first time I had ever heard the term, "Scrambler." They need to spread out, brace their rumps against something, and they like a lot of room. Sue gave

Clifford a shot of Banamine and talked to him softly. Then she turned to me and said, "YOU need to calm down. You two are too connected."

After talking with her and hearing about how she had successfully showed a horse, traveling all over the country, who had the same problem, I began to think that there was some hope. And there was great comfort in naming it and knowing something could be done for him.

But she was right. I was terribly shaky. After some deliberation, we decided to go on to the expo, because it was closer than home, and there was sure to be a vet there. We took it slow, and with the partition out, he did not go down again. He unloaded nicely but was still very stressed, as was I. He had whacked his knee, and it was swollen twice its size, and despite having a blanket on, he had torn a pancake-sized chunk of hide off his hip. It was rather embarrassing having the Morgan ambassador showing up looking as if he'd been in a bar fight. He was sleepy-eyed the rest of that long day. The vet came and looked at him, tubed him so he wouldn't colic, and had me walk him around. She said he would be fine to do his tricks the next day, he was just sore. She suggested some Bute and said the Banamine would help too.

The next morning he was eating, sweet and quiet, not at all himself. He wasn't greeting people with his usual interest. He was far too polite to everyone. He did perk up when the dogs did their tricks, showing some interest in earning goodies. But when we went out into the arena, I turned him loose as was our tradition, and he immediately trotted to the gate and asked to go back to his stall. The crowd laughed, sympathetically, and it took a little coaxing to get him to free lead for treats. He loved the cone retrieve, but for the first time in his life, he did not get the cone. He walked a few steps and then just stopped and stood there. More sympathetic laughter.

"Okay," I said. I clipped the lead rope back on him and picked up the cone. I hated walking out of there without him finishing the trick, so I tossed it a couple of feet. He just looked at it. I picked it up, led him a few steps, then tossed it again. To humor me, he picked it up and delivered it, to half-hearted applause.

He returned to the stall and I took the brush, and groomed and babied him. I took the cone and had him pick it up in the stall a few times. Then, as the day wore on, four hours after his turn in the arena, I went into his stall with the manure fork. Someone paused to ask, "How old is he? What is a Morgan like?" And as I stood describing how fun their personalities are, as if to confirm it, Clifford tried to grab the manure fork and he bonked me in the head with the handle.

I turned and looked at him. His eyes snapped with a hint of roguish fun.

"Hey!" I said. "You feel better!"

The show was closing. The arena was empty. I put his halter back on and led him out into the arena. I had him do a couple of easy things, stack, back up and walk and stop. He earned clicks and treats. He was kind of half-heartedly cooperative, so I picked up the cone. I turned him loose.

Our booth neighbors with the Icelandic pony were wandering through and they said, "OH! We've got to see Clifford!"

"Well," I explained, "He's not really himself today."

"Oh that's okay!" They beamed.

Normally he cued me when he was ready to get the cone. He would drop his head and put his ears up. I had trained this because I wanted him to concentrate, with forward ears, and not look crabby as is his wont at times. That day, he did not drop his head. His eyes were kind of wandering. I shook the cone a little, and he looked at it, and put his head down.

"Okay." I tossed it.

He ambled over, picked it up, and brought it back. CLICK! And a big treat. It wasn't his usual explosive departure, nor his vigorous return, but it was something. The Icelandic people cheered.

Clifford went to the gate and asked to be excused. I didn't want this to be his idea. I took a chance that he might refuse the cone again, but I coaxed him back for a second retrieve. I could imagine that it was hurting him to move, and he probably had bruises I didn't even know about. But he came back. I shook the cone. He dropped his head, ears cupped forward. He was primed.

I flung that cone, and it sailed off, and he took off and trotted after it. He picked it up, I clicked, and he turned. I started running backward, whooping and yelling. The Icelandic people yelled. Clifford tossed his head and came barreling back with that cone just like he was supposed to do.

"YAYYYYY!!!" I said, and gave him a big piece of candy. I quickly snapped the lead rope on him and we left the arena.

We went back to the stall. "Good boy," I said, scratching and hugging him.

As I removed his halter, a man sitting next to my booth said, "That is amazing. I have never, ever seen a horse do that."

"Oh, you saw the retrieve from here?" I turned, and noticed his vantage point and that he could indeed see the arena.

"Yes, it was great!"

"Well, it wasn't his best," I explained. "He is not himself today."

"Oh?"

"Yeah." I went on to explain about our horrendous trailer experience of the day before.

The man stared at me. "You mean, he went through all that just yesterday, and he's actually here doing this stuff right now?"

I hesitated. And it suddenly dawned on me that he was right! I was asking a heck of a lot from this traumatized horse.

"Wow. I never thought about it that way." I turned and looked at Clifford. He lifted his head and rested his nose against my cheek. Then he went back to munching his hay.

The next morning I hurried into a convenience store.

"Do you have any StarBrite mints?"

"What?" The clerk looked at me.

"StarBrites! StarBrites! I need StarBrite peppermints!"

"Oh!" he brightened, pointing to a rack with candy at the end of the aisle. "Right over there."

I bought two packages. I figured I'd need them. Clifford was waiting hungrily in his stall when I arrived. The swelling had gone down in his knee due to the anti-inflammatory Sue Hall had given him. He seemed more like himself, too, though he was obviously still very sore.

In the back of my mind that day, of course, was the question of how he was going to do on the ride home. I called Dr. Robinson who had tubed him on Friday, and she agreed to come out and give him something to calm him before he was loaded. Martha Edwards, a Morgan person who organized Clifford's appearance at the Expo, stopped by and gave me her phone number and insisted that I call her if anything happened. She offered the suggestion of putting shavings from his stall in the trailer -- apparently a standard thing which again, I had not known.

Despite this nagging tension, the day was pleasant enough due to the well wishes of various Morgan folk. Clifford, munching hay, appreciated all the attention, gravitating especially toward small children who stopped to see him. He received a lot of compliments on his pretty head, despite the scrape over his one eye. I guess people liked the Pirate look.

As his performance time grew closer, I noticed Clifford pacing back and forth in his stall, cocking one ear toward me, watching me intently. He was starting to nicker to me, looking over people's heads at me when they stopped to pet him, and seeming agitated. I realized suddenly that it was because I was agitated! I was flitting back and forth behind my table, gathering treats for my fanny pack, straightening literature on display, and generally fussing as I thought about our upcoming performance. As I paced and turned, so did he.

I realized then how clear Sue Hall's perception had been, about us being "connected." I thought I'd better relax a little. I sat down, but he kept watching me. He knew something was up.

Finally our turn came. I had decided to work him on a longe line instead of trying to free longe him this time. I clipped the longe onto him, opened his stall door and he burst forward ahead of me eagerly. We went down the aisle toward the arena. His ears were up and he seemed okay. I showed him my bagful of peppermints. Peppermints were my ace in the hole -- the thing I used as a jackpot for his best performances. When he did acceptably well, he got apples or grain or cookies, but for the retrieve, when he'd really shine, he earned a peppermint. That day I carried nothing but peppermints!

I led him into the arena, stacked him and he stretched his neck beautifully for the audience, earning a click and a treat. I could hear Logan Hyatt's recorded "Linus and Lucy", the music I had selected last year. As the announcer talked about Figure and the origins of the Morgan breed, I let the longe play out and urged him into a trot. He stepped forward, moving a little stiffly, but with great enthusiasm. I could see he was excited, and I kept looking at that big pancake-shaped mark on his hip. I had spray painted over it with chestnut-colored horsy show stuff, but it was still pretty obvious.

I was picturing the announcer saying, "Please excuse this horse's appearance and uncharacteristically nervous behavior. He has had a rough weekend."

The audience was silent, but when I glanced over, they were smiling. And I realized that Clifford really was beautiful, and that is something I'd forget when living with him. He was such a person to me that I didn't think about it. Maybe this time he didn't need to do free leading or tricks -- maybe for now just this was enough. I told him to stop, and he did, and then we turned and longed the other direction while the announcer talked about Morgans and all the things they could do today.

As the description of Morgans ended, I led Clifford back to the gate and grabbed the cone. I unhooked him and he followed me back a few steps. His head wasn't all the way down, but I took a chance and pitched the cone toward the center of the arena. He bolted forward and as I held my breath, he picked it up. I clicked and then ran backwards and yelled to him. He barrelled toward me carrying the cone and then placed it in my hand. I grabbed his halter and led him out the gate to a small smattering of applause. I was glad they didn't erupt as they had in previous years, as that had scared him. I was so proud of him and so grateful for his honesty and courage! When we went back to the stall, I patted and hugged him, and gave him ALL the remaining peppermints.

"We're going home!" I whispered to him.

After that, I felt better and was optimistic about the trip home. Dr. Robinson showed up as promised and gave him a shot. I don't even know what it was. With the partition out and whatever he was on, he did just fine.

He unloaded in the light, misty rain, and was greeted by his sister Trudy, and went back into his own warm stall.

Chapter Thirty-Three

*"I found I could say things with color and shapes
that I couldn't say any other way -
things I had no words for."*
~ Georgia O'Keeffe

I had heard somewhere that amputees think the missing limb is still there. When they look and see it gone, it is a surprise, over and over.

My house was filled with reminders of Kim. Photos, stuffed animals she had sent me over the years. Her stenciled wood paintings hung on my walls. Things that were fixtures in my life now leaped out as constant reminders that she was gone.

Her already faltering world had collapsed when her husband had left. She couldn't hold it together on her own, and she had never recovered. I was terrified that, once my alimony ran out, the same would happen to me. I feared that Bruce had been right – that I was a "Nothing", that I was useless. I was mightily scared and, as the months went by, I was only becoming more confused about what to do.

Kim was gone. But memories of her were invariably combined with her encouragement, and her reminders of the one thing I could do well.

I found the red tin box of paints in a dark closet, covered in a layer of dust like a thin shroud of discouragement. I had a collection of thick watercolor paper, tablets and pads in various sizes. Some had been gently used, some were still wrapped tightly in cellophane. The set of watercolors remained in its box, tubes lined up according to color. They had hardly been touched.

That winter I opened them.

I poured my grief out into colors that mixed and blended and flowed onto the paper. I spent hours laboring over lines, moving paint with brushes, escaping into the intricacy of each piece. I learned that watercolors were much more versatile than I'd imagined. They carried more impact than I thought, when using layer upon layer. They required patience.

And they were forgiving.

As I worked, I experienced that sort of zen that happens when one is concentrating; that satisfaction brought on by a simple effort. I thought about Clifford overcoming his pain and trauma at the Expo, and how he had forged ahead, how going through the motions seemed to make him feel better. I remembered our clicker sessions, when he learned to wait with his ears forward, and his attitude had improved.

The act itself had caused his emotions to follow.

I thought of Patty, how she had beat the odds and lived so much longer than was predicted, just by showing up for work every day. I thought of Scorch climbing up an agility A frame, even though he obsessively worried about his feet. I thought of Reva, and how no matter what, even in the midst of dying, her mindset was to just keep going, keep doing.

Maybe that was the trick; the secret to recovery. I had always thought I needed to somehow be mentally prepared for things. Maybe it was the doing of the thing that would prepare me.

I put my brush down and dialed the phone. When I heard a voice crackle on the line, I said, "Jacki, this is Nancy. Do you have room for Trudy again this year?"

Chapter Thirty-Four

*"Whatever it is given you to do,
do it with all your heart."*
~ Jesus Christ

"You make me young again," Amanda said when we were driving back from the Soo with our sister-in-law, Judy. We had just enjoyed a girl's day out. The three of us occasionally went to the movies and then to Anggio's for pizza.

"We make you young again? What are you talking about? You're only thirty-three!" I looked at her in the rearview mirror. She was sitting in the back seat with her beige raincoat on, her wig tipped back on her forehead to reveal the gently emerging lines there.

She slapped a pudgy hand up to her face. "I don't want to think about it."

"Amanda!" Judy said. "Thirty-three is young!"

"Someone's got a birthday coming up," I said knowingly.

"Don't MENTION it!" Amanda moaned.

Amanda's birthday was September 24th. The leaves were turning that aged green color that would eventually meld into gold. I had spent the summer working on watercolors. I had put the first one up for sale on eBay, an online auction site. To my surprise, someone bought it. Others followed. My sales were sporadic and I was just getting by, but at least the animals and I weren't starving.

That summer had been a brief one, cold and rainy, with several trips to Drummond. Trudy stayed in training with Jacki. I didn't have the nerve to haul Clifford that year. It was the first time in ten years that he didn't go North, and it rained on the Fourth of July parade.

I didn't go to Clifford's Bay. I couldn't bear to look at the mangled trees.

Amanda worked full time at the Drummond Island Laundry and Linen Rental, washing and folding sheets and towels for the resorts on the Island. She worked hard and came home exhausted, and I hadn't been around much for her. Things were changing for all of us.

"Look at me! I'm forty-two," I said.

"I'm over fifty!" Judy chimed in. "Amanda, you're the youngest of us all!"

"Yep, you're just a puppy," I said.

"Yeah, right," she looked out the window.

Amanda was a hard-core birthday connoisseur. They were important events to her. Not just hers, either. If she knew someone as more than just an acquaintance, she knew when their birthday was. She also could name the year and sometimes even the time of day they had come into the world.

Since her thirtieth birthday, I had noticed her having a little harder time with each one. I guessed that was normal.

The weeks passed and it seemed before I knew it, the end of September was upon us. I of course made the trip North, with gifts and a card. I sat down at the kitchen table that night with Amanda, and asked, "What do you want to do for your birthday tomorrow?"

She had an answer ready. "I want to go up on a bluff and shout out our ages."

I was eating a sandwich, and I paused in mid-bite. "Really?"

"Yes. You know, up over the houses and people, up high, and shout so everyone can hear."

I nodded. "Okay."

The next day we drove to the Soo with Judy. We went to the movies, and out to Ang-gio's. We sat in a booth waiting for our pizza and Amanda said, "I put something in your purse, Nancy."

"You did?"

My bag had been sitting in the back seat with her. I unzipped it and dug through it, and pulled out a party favor – a bright pink whistle that unfurled when it was blown into.

"Judy's got one too," Amanda said.

Judy looked in her purse and, sure enough, she also had a whistle. Amanda reached into her own bag and held up an identical one.

"Wow," I said. "You really plan ahead."

"On three," Amanda said.

We all held the whistles poised to our lips. Amanda held up one finger, then two, then a third. We blew, hard, and a loud squealing rose from our table as the whistles unfurled and jostled together. Other diners looked over and smiled.

"Happy birthday, Amanda!" I said.

"Happy birthday! Happy birthday!" Judy agreed.

Amanda beamed. We devoured our pizza and laughed and joked, and then the waitress emerged with a cake and a single lit candle on top.

"Look at this!" I said. I hadn't told them it was her birthday, but someone must have noticed the fuss we were making.

"Isn't that nice of them?" Judy said.

"We have to sing."

Amanda covered her face as Judy and I brayed an off-key version of, "Happy Birthday To You" as loud as we could. But I could see that she was smiling.

We left the restaurant, and I drove us up to the campus of Lake Superior State University, where I had attended college years before. Behind the Student Services building, there was an enormous hill that overlooked the International Bridge to Canada. We pulled up alongside some small maples and looked out over the expanse of city far below that was Sault Canada, and the Sault Locks where the big freighters came through. A light breeze blew across the hill from Lake Superior to the west of us.

"This must be the bluff!" Judy said.

"This is it!" We jumped out of the car and walked across the grass, among the young maple trees, to the edge of the tremendous steep hill. We were indeed looking down upon the "houses and people".

I turned to Amanda. "Here we are. You have to go first. It's your birthday."

She didn't hesitate. She took a deep breath and roared with all her might. "I'm THIRTY-FOUR! THIRTY-FOUR! I'm THIRTY-FOUR YEARS OLD!"

Judy and I looked at each other, a little startled. We hadn't expected such vocal power from such a little person.

I jumped forward, hopping up and down and flinging my arms up over my head. "I'm TWENTY-NINE! I'm TWENTY-NINE!"

Judy's voice broke with laughter as she wailed, "I'M TWENTY-SIX!"

"Okay," Amanda said. "I'M TWENTY-FIVE! I'M TWENTY-FIVE!"

"WOO HOO! YEAH!" I yelled, clapping my hands, and we all leaped and cheered, shouting over the rooftops, into the air toward the setting sun.

Chapter Thirty-Five

"Faith is a passionate intuition."
~ William Wordsworth

The red trailer was possessed. "Wheelzebub", I had dubbed it. It hunkered at the level spot beside the garage, looking innocent enough, but I knew better. I had parked it there after dropping Trudy off at Jacki's in the spring. While unhitching it, I forgot to block the wheels. I blithely cranked the hitch away until it popped off the ball. With a groan, it eased backward away from the truck. I still had ahold of the crank handle, and when I realized that it was getting away from me, I pulled hard. It stopped, and I stood there, holding on to it. But gravity was pulling against me. The trailer was determined to go down the slope. I tried to hang on, to slow its descent, but it got the best of me and finally I let go. It rolled down the hill, circled around the apple tree, and crashed through the fence. The wires snapped and whirled through the air. Midway through the fence, Wheelzebub stopped and rested there triumphantly among the remnants of wire.

The fence was repaired later. From then on I knew enough to block the wheels. I realized that most of our trailering incidents had been my own fault, but I thought there was still something creepy about it. I didn't blame Clifford for his issues with it.

One afternoon I opened up the trailer and began cleaning it out, preparing to put fresh shavings in it for Trudy's trip home. I heard a neigh, and turned to see Clifford watching me from a spot by the barn.

I looked around. The partition was still out from our Novi incident the autumn before. I had hauled Trudy to Jacki's without bothering to put it back in. Wheelzebub was, essentially, a one-horse trailer.

Clifford stood looking at me.

"Do you want to try this?" I went to the barn and got his halter. Cajun and Scorch leaped around me joyously. Clifford stuck his head in the halter and followed me up the hill. He walked right into the trailer and stood there expectantly.

"Okay," I said. "Let's hitch it up."

It was a sunny October day and I decided to drive ten miles down the road to where the Lakeland Trail, a revamped railroad, crossed into the woods.

I put Clifford's saddle in the back of the truck and we were off. I drove slowly, creeping down the steep hill with the window down, listening intently for any kicking sounds. When I reached the first stop sign, I got out, walked around and looked in on him. He was standing sideways in the trailer, looking back out at me. I remembered what the Animal Communicator, Judy Long, had said about Clifford wanting to be on the right. He had in fact always been leaning to the right, and now he stood with his rump braced against the right wall

"You okay?"

He seemed fine.

I drove on. We pulled up in a parking lot near the trail and I unloaded Clifford. He had not even broken a sweat.

"You mean that's all you wanted? Just to stand sideways?"

I saddled him up. The dogs were ecstatic. I had only ridden twice that year, and that was just around the house. But now, even though he was fat and out of shape, Clifford burst forward and trotted energetically down the trail. His ears were up.

We rode for an hour, through the crisp fluttering leaves, scaring up a blue heron in the creek below the trail, and watching some wild geese winging overhead. The dogs trotted ahead of us, stopping to sniff in the grass here and there. Clifford moved with his usual springy trot, looking around with bright cheerful interest. I remembered how much he loved to go, and I realized that I did too. I had neglected him and myself. My fear had caused me to lose this important part of our lives. It was time to stop postponing things.

Clifford rode home without incident. When I got him settled in his stall with some grain, I went in the house and dialed the phone. "Jacki? I want to enter Trudy in a show."

Chapter Thirty-Six

"Do the thing, and you shall have the power."
~ Ralph Waldo Emerson

Jacki had entered Trudy in a small all-breed show at Shiawassee County Fairgrounds. The show barn smelled of fresh shavings that Friday afternoon. I was surprised by the lack of activity, though horses called to each other now and then and the air had an anticipatory snap to it. I walked up the aisle and which had folding chairs scattered here and there, but there was no sign of anyone. Horses peered at me from the stalls.

"Hi!" a voice said. I looked over and there was Jacki, in one stall brushing her stallion, B.C. He was in cross ties and blinked at me brightly.

"Hi Jacki! How's it going?"

"Trudy's not a happy camper."

"She's not?"

"She's scared."

"Where is she?"

Jacki nodded toward the row of stalls and I walked down to see Trudy standing with her face in the corner. I opened up the stall door and went in. "Hi Tude! What's up?"

She turned and I could see the surprise registering in her eyes. Perhaps she thought I had abandoned her to be auctioned off in this place. Perhaps she thought I was never coming back. Whatever she thought, she hadn't expected to see me. She began nibbling softly up and down my arms, a quiet greeting. Tension simmered from her, tight like a rubber band.

I had my fanny pack on, filled with cut up bits of apple. I reached in and pulled my clicker out. I hadn't brought the target stick, so held out my left hand instead and said, "Touch."

She immediately touched my palm softly with her warm muzzle. I clicked and gave her a piece of apple. As she chewed it, I held my hand out again. "Touch."

Again she touched it, received another treat, and then I took a step to the side, causing her to take a step to follow me. Now her mind was on the job. The entire summer had gone without her doing any clicker training. I imagined it was a comfort to her, the old routine, the communication so clear to her.

We repeated the process. Touch, click, treat. Touch, click, treat. I slowly backed around the stall, making her take small steps, and lowering my hand each time until her nose was practically on the ground. As she circled with her head down, way down, in the natural relaxed position of a horse before it rolls, the tension left her.

She stood then, with her head dropped, and I petted and talked to her. "It's just a show. I'm going to lead you around the ring! And then Jacki will drive you later. It's all the same stuff you know already. You'll see."

She heaved a big breath, a loose and gentle snort. She was all right.

"I wanted to drive her around the arena today, to give her an idea of what to expect and see how she feels." Jacki said.

"That's a good idea!"

It quickly dawned on me that things were out of my hands. Jacki's friends Chris and Pat helped put the harness on Trudy. When Jacki led her out into the sunshine, they grabbed the shafts and pulled the cart on and hooked her up. I stood by with my camera, watching the process. Jacki climbed into the cart and clucked to her, and they were off. The cart rolled and jounced softly as Trudy clipped down the dirt road past the outbuildings and around the park. I took photos. The sun bounced off the little mare and Jacki's long braid swung behind her.

Jacki slowed her to a walk.

"She's so cute!" Pat said.

Trudy was always a thing of beauty, with her proud head and glossy dark coat. But when hitched to a cart, she seemed to really have found her niche. Her hocks and knees lifted daintily. Her mane and tail flowed and her muscles rippled. She was embracing the thing she had feared the most, and for a moment I thought of Amanda, standing on a bluff, shouting out her age.

Jacki turned the mare and cart, and headed for the arena. "Okay! We're going in!"

They took off up the gentle slope and in through the gate. I ran after them, and as I watched Trudy trot up the rail, I stopped. I caught my breath. She flew around the arena confidently, with the cart whizzing behind her.

The cart squeaked, the harness jingled a bit, and Trudy's hoofs thumped into the sand in a muffled rhythm. She turned and passed behind us, then came up the other side for another pass. Her glossy neck was arched, her trot was free and straight. Her polished hoofs flashed in the soft light. She was perfection.

"How's she look?" Jacki said.

"She looks great!" Chris said. "Really nice!"

I couldn't speak. All I could do was stand there in the center of the arena, turning slowly with my forgotten camera in my hand, as I watched with tears pouring down my face.

The mare had recovered. Even without the competition, she was showing me that nothing was too big or scary – no accident, no loss, no journey. Even her fear from earlier today was completely gone. It didn't matter what happened from here. This was her moment. She was showing me what moxie was – and she was doing it beautifully.

Jacki directed her to the center of the arena and stopped. I stepped up to take the bridle. I stood close to her, feeling her warm breath on my hand. My face was drenched with tears. I couldn't speak.

"Are you having a meltdown?" Jacki said, noticing my face. I nodded and she laughed.

"Okay, we're done," she clucked to Trudy and they trotted out.

I started to follow but Chris stopped me.

"Hang on there. Just give yourself a few minutes. Don't worry. She's okay."

Actually I wasn't worried. There was so much more to it, but it was far too much to explain.

"It just won't do her any good to have you emotional like this. It will affect her, make her nervous." She patted my arm and smiled. "You've got your mare back."

I nodded. That was true. And maybe I was getting myself back too.

When Trudy was back in her stall, I went back into the barn and Jacki handed me a pile of leather that was the harness. "Here," she said. "Would you mind cleaning this?"

"Oh, not at all!" I was happy to have something to do. A tack box that lay in the empty stall designated for grooming. I took a rag and a bottle of leather cleaner and sat down to wipe the seemingly endless mass of straps and buckles.

"Trudy looked great out there," Chris said. She sat not far from me, watching the process.

I smiled. "Yeah, she did. Oh, yuck. Look at that bit."

The bit was covered with slime, horsey saliva. There was a water bottle sitting by my feet and I picked it up and began busily spritzing the metal bars.

"Um, I think that might be fly spray in that bottle," Chris said.

"Oh no!" I held the bottle up and smelled it. Sure enough. Strong, pungent and toxic fly spray now coated the bit, dripping off it in rivulets.

"I'd better go rinse this off." I stood up and carried the bridle outside as Chris politely stifled a giggle.

I carried the bridle around the corner to the wash rack and as I rinsed it, I noticed a group of women hosing down a waist-high pinto pony.

"He's cute!" I said. "What class is he in?"

"Pleasure driving," they replied.

"Oh, he'll be up against my mare! I'll see you there."

When I came back with the bridle, Trudy was in the stall designated as a grooming area, cross tied with three women working on her, brushing her and spritzing her and painting her hoofs a glossy black. Her coat was polished to a dramatic sheen. She rolled a dark and trusting eye at me as I walked up.

My friend Gina stood leaning in the doorway, dressed in a black coat and pants. Gina had an experienced Morgan breeder for many years. She had offered to be the "tailer", the one who follows the horse with a whip and makes sure that the horse is working off its hindquarters in the ring. It also adds a little show "spark" to most horses at the idea of being "chased."

I would have the job of leading her. As we all walked out into the sunshine that morning, Trudy glowed. I could not imagine a horse more beautiful. Her neck was arched, her delicate head adorned with the gleaming leather bridle, brow band shining in burgundy and gold.

"Here," Jacki handed me the reins. "Take her out and walk her around a bit. Let her get the feel of that bridle."

Trudy bumped and jostled me. I kept poking her with my elbow. "She's too close. She's gonna step on me."

"It's best if you hold the bar on that bit," Jacki said. "That way you can keep her where you want her, and she'll feel more secure too."

I took the bar in my hand. We walked around. I felt as if I had a dance partner. Trudy floated beside me, with her freshly unbraided tail drifting through the air in gentle waves.

"This is better," I said.

"Okay, when you get in the ring, just start running. The horses will be moving at a pretty good clip. She'll have to trot around the ring counter-clockwise and then line up on that opposite wall."

"That's when I'll take her and stand her up for you." Gina said.

"They are all bigger than she is." I looked around. There were several stretchy mares walking and jigging around the area with handlers. The air was electric with anticipation.

"They're Saddlebreds," Jacki said. "This judge is a Saddlebred judge."

The gate swung open and I heard the announcer's voice calling for Open Mares.

"That's your cue," Gina said. "Go!"

Trudy and I were off. I knew that even though she was a little mare, Trudy's trot was formidable, so I stretched my legs and ran. She moved with me easily and had no trouble staying in line with the taller horses.

We circled the arena. I heard Gina's husband Logan playing the organ, some bright lively tune that blended with the controlled excitement of the show ring.

We stopped at the opposite side of the arena where the mares lined up. Gina came over and took the bridle. She put one hand on Trudy's shoulder and pushed her back. I stepped away. Trudy's head went up and her eyes rolled in confusion. She emitted an ear-splitting neigh.

"Stand up, Mare," Gina said softly. Trudy's feet lined up, but she thrust her sides out away from Gina so she was standing in a sort of U-shape. She whinnied again, her body shivering violently with the effort.

The judge, a sweetly smiling lady dressed in grey, walked past us, giving Trudy the once-over. Trudy bellered again.

"Be quiet!" I hissed.

I looked around. Trudy was completely different from the other mares in the class. She was much darker in color, more compact, with smaller ears, larger eyes and a rounded frame. Her neck was much more cresty. The others were tall, leggy, and everything about them was long. Long ears. Long noses. Long, lean torsos. The scene reminded me of a child's workbook, where they would line up pictures of many oranges and then a single apple, with the question, "Which of these does not belong?"

The judge went back to the front of the line. "Okay, take her," Gina handed me the bridle.

As soon as I took the bit, Trudy's head dropped and I felt the tension abruptly leave her. She didn't know Gina, and this was all completely new to her.

"It's okay, Tude," I said. "This is just for fun. No pressure."

Around the ring we trotted again. I knew that Trudy was representing the Morgan breed, and she was beautiful. Happy to be back in my care, she arched her neck and shook her mane a bit, as if she understood. When we reached the end I scratched her gratefully on the withers. At home she was Trudy, my sweet girl. Here, she was an equine work of art. I couldn't believe that she actually belonged to me. I felt blessed.

The announcer called the numbers of various other horses. We had not placed.

As I led her from the ring, I was surprised by the grumblings in our group. They were disappointed. Jacki said she should have placed higher.

But I remembered that release of tension I had felt when I took the bit from Gina in the show ring. I remembered the way Trudy had relaxed when I had spoken to her, secure in the knowledge that all was well. Even with Kimmy gone, someone still believed in me.

"It's okay," I said. "She looks great! That's what matters."

"That judge likes them big," Jacki said.

"Well," I chirped happily. "We are up against that little pony in Open Driving, so that might be a good thing!"

"Not any more!" Jacki said. "We're through with this Open stuff! We're going back to Morgans!"

So that afternoon, we hitched her up and Jacki donned a glittery striped jacket and climbed into the show cart. She drove without hesitation into the ring. Trudy arched her neck and trotted. There was no competition. She was the only horse in the class.

Logan was still playing the keyboard, and naturally privy to the whole situation. I had to laugh when I suddenly recognized his message for Trudy through the music. He was pounding out the Beatles tune, "Get Back to Where You Once Belonged"!

Everyone was pulling for Trudy. Other Morgan people who had heard the story of our accident came to line up and watch, and encourage her to, "Get Back."

And she did. She trotted, walked and then parked out in the center of the ring, and even backed up when the judge asked for it. She got her blue ribbon and posed and had her picture taken. We clapped for her.

I was thrilled. Everyone kept telling me how cute she was. And she had a blue ribbon, after all!

But I had a persistent notion that the show wasn't over for us.

And then Jacki asked her good friend Jon Sweet to try Trudy in Classic Pleasure Driving. Jon was a farrier and trainer, and owner of Sugarlane Morgan Farm. He had been breeding and showing Morgans for many years. He agreed to do it.

"He can DRIVE!" Jacki whispered to me, with a nudge.

I was so excited by the prospect of Trudy having another go, and with a new driver to boot. The experience with someone else driving her could only be good for her. That afternoon Jon, a powerfully built man with a gentle nature, pulled Trudy's shoes, removing the pads and replacing the plates, which were consistent with the show regulations. He donned a dapper coat and hat and climbed into the cart. After a couple of passes outside, they were off.

There was another mare in the class, and she was easily over fifteen hands. Knowing the judge's preference, I didn't harbor any false hopes.

As Trudy trotted confidently along the rail, Jacki said, "Well, now I get to watch her! Jeez, they told me she looked good, but I never knew she looked THAT good!"

All around me people were remarking on the mare's natural hock action, huge stride and beautiful classic Morgan features. Trudy appeared to be in her element. In fact, as she passed me at the road trot, I yelled, "TUDE!" as I used to do when really asking her to fly, during our old driving days up on Drummond.

I thought I saw the surprise registering on Jon's face at that moment. He later said, "I was trying to hold her back, because I know she is little. But she didn't want to be held back. Then when they asked for a road trot, I let her go, but she just kept giving me more!"

The two mares lined up, and Jacki ran out to stand at Trudy's head. She was asked to back, again, which she did with no problem.

The tension rose as the mares stood in the dusty arena, the evening light angling through the cart wheels as the judge moved around them. Then the announcer's voice cracked over the loudspeaker. "The winner of class 40, Classic Pleasure Driving, is number 237, Kerry Aira-"

"SHE DID IT!" I screamed. I was leaping up and down, shouting her name, Airatude, AIR-A-TUDE! People all around me were cheering, laughing and applauding.

She had done it. Jacki had brought her from a dark place of confusion and panic, and after long and careful rehabilitation, Trudy had gone into a show -- something she had never done before -- and won.

I felt as if she was sending me a message, and I was reading it loud and clear. It was my turn.

Chapter Thirty-Seven

"When you face the sun, the shadows fall behind you."
~ Helen Keller

I pulled Wheelzebub up Jacki's driveway, listening to the gravel crunch beneath the tires. We were enjoying a long awaited bit of summer. As I opened the truck door, I noticed the way the light was bouncing off the clouds, giving them body and substance like big, puffy animals.

I walked into the barn and saw that Trudy already stood waiting patiently in harness, cross tied in her stall. Jacki greeted me, smiling. Her eyes sparkled a little. I could tell she was excited for us, and I felt a sudden surge of gratitude to her.

She unhooked Trudy and led her down the barn aisle into the arena where Tammi waited with the cart. Trudy was hitched quickly and without incident.

Jacki had attached some long cotton training reins that trailed behind the cart. She picked them up and rolled them into a ball, laying them on the seat. "You have to sit on these, to keep them from dragging. But if they do fall out and drag, it's all right. It's not going to mess you up or anything. They'll stay behind you."

She walked over and stood by the mare's head, holding the bridle. "Okay, you ready?"

I was a little surprised that Jacki didn't want to drive her first, just to see how she was that day. But it didn't bother me. It was Jacki's implicit message, her confidence that all was well. I could feel Trudy's readiness, her eagerness to move on. The future sprawled before us, inviting, bright and full of possibilities.

I climbed in without hesitation and took up the reins as Jacki stepped back, smiling. The reins were soft in my hands, and I could feel the familiar tension of the mare's gentle mouth on the other end. I nodded to Jacki and gave Trudy a light tap.

"Okay!" I said as we moved forward. "Let's go!"